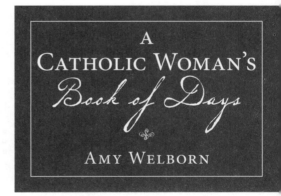

A CATHOLIC WOMAN'S Book of Days

AMY WELBORN

LOYOLAPRESS.

CHICAGO

LOYOLAPRESS.

3441 N. ASHLAND AVENUE
CHICAGO, ILLINOIS 60657
(800) 621-1008
WWW.LOYOLABOOKS.ORG

The Scripture quotations contained herein cited are from the New Revised Standard Version Bible: Catholic Edition, copyright © 1993 and 1989 by the Division of Christian Education of the National Council of the Churches of Christ in the U.S.A. Used by permission. All rights reserved.

Suscipe is from *The Spiritual Exercises of St. Ignatius of Loyola,* trans. Louis J. Puhl, S.J. (Chicago: Loyola University Press, 1951).

Cover photography by Phil Martin

Cross collection courtesy of Vineyard Books, Gifts & Church Supplies, Rockford, Illinois (www.catholicfamilygifts.com)

Cover and interior design by Laura Steur

Library of Congress Cataloging-in-Publication Data
Welborn, Amy.
  A Catholic woman's book of days / Amy Welborn.
        p. cm.
  ISBN 0-8294-2057-6
  1. Catholic women—Prayer-books and devotions—English.   2. Devotional calendars—Catholic Church.   I. Title.
BX2170.W7W45   2005
242'.643—dc22
                                                          2004028741

Printed in the United States of America
05 06 07 08 09 10 Bang 10 9 8 7 6 5 4 3 2

Introduction

In the course of a day, a week, or a year, each of us is touched by God in ways too numerous to count and often too profound to explain. If we're honest we might also admit that, as hopeful as we might be about God's active presence in our lives, we're often far too busy to notice it.

In *A Catholic Woman's Book of Days,* I've tried to offer daily meditations that clear a spiritual space in which to recognize that Presence, no matter how busy the rest of life is. These thoughts are rooted in my own experiences, but I hope that the moments on which I reflect and the questions that I ask are broad enough to include yours, too.

As we journey through this year together, may our hearts be enlivened by God's constant grace, our spirits be freed in his mercy and love, and our whole beings grow more finely tuned to the Lord's presence—within every sentence and page of the "book of days" called life.

January

January 1

But Mary treasured all these words
and pondered them in her heart.

—Luke 2:19

The previous months had given Mary much to contemplate: her mysterious, God-given pregnancy; her aged cousin's maternity; and the birth of her Son attended—marvelously—by angels.

The beginning of a new year is the natural time to reflect on the past. But let's be careful to sift through these memories of joy and regret in the right way.

Reflecting on the past helps us discern God's will and how we've responded to it. It can hurt, though, if our reflections become occasions for paralyzing regret or wishful nostalgia, both of which blind us to God's presence in the here and now, in the limitless possibility of the brand-new year.

Lord, thank you for the past year of my life. Help me to grow in my awareness of your love in the present moment and not be discouraged by the past.

January 2

Let what you heard from the
beginning abide in you.
—1 JOHN 2:24

What is it you have heard from the beginning?
For many of us, childhood memories of religious formation are suffused with a sense of simple trust. Our parents, grandparents, and teachers told us that God created us, loves us, and takes care of us.

It's good to remember that those who taught us to trust knew, as we do now, of suffering, pain, and shadows. These experiences may have raised questions, but they also, in the end, brought the answers of trust and faith they shared with us.

Lord, in this new year, give me the grace to live in response to the simple truth of your love and care for me.

O sing to the LORD a new song,
for he has done marvelous things.

—PSALM 98:1

The baby sits in the middle of his super-duper play saucer, propped upright by a towel around his middle, his feet dangling in the air. His eyes are wide open, and his head just can't stop moving as his gaze darts from toy to toy.

Within seconds, he starts wailing. It's all just too much. The wealth of amusing and developmentally helpful plastic objects has overwhelmed him with choices.

As the new year begins and we contemplate what we want to make of it, our reaction may be similar to the baby's. Evidence of our faults surrounds us, and opportunities for growth and change overwhelm us. Which way should we go? What should come first?

The psalmist gives us a different idea. Instead of beginning with self-scrutiny, why not start this year with a new song: one of openhearted praise?

Lord, I thank you for my life and for the chance to grow that this new year brings.

January 4

When Jesus turned and saw them following, he
said to them, "What are you looking for?"

—JOHN 1:38

Mo re times than I care to admit, I stride into a
room or up the stairs with a great air of purpose
and then come to a stop, bewildered. I haven't a clue as
to why I'm there.

What in the world was I looking for?

If Jesus were to stop us in the middle of our confident daily journeys from room to room, meeting to
meeting, and goal to goal and ask us the question he
poses to the disciples here, would we have an answer?

*Lord, help me look at my life today and discern what
it is I'm looking for.*

January 5

Nathanael said to him, "Can anything
good come out of Nazareth?"
Philip said to him, "Come and see."

—JOHN 1:46

Want to succeed? That's easy. Gather up your stunning résumé, your magna cum laude degree, your stellar references, and your fabulous good looks.

Thank heaven that's not what God is looking for.

Just run down the list of his choices. From the young (David, Jeremiah) to the awkward (Moses) to the reluctant (just about everyone), hardly any of them have résumés that would impress.

Especially a carpenter's son from that backwater called Nazareth.

To know that God works through those the world scorns should be a great comfort to us.

Lord, today I present myself, weakness and strength, wisdom and foolishness. Use me as I am to do your will.

January 6

I too decided, after investigating everything
carefully from the very first, to write an
orderly account for you.

—LUKE 1:3

At the age of eight, my daughter developed a keen
interest in whether the books she read were
"true stories." She was wondering if there might be
something about a not-true story that made it less
worthy of her time.

Imagine her joy when, after many tries, she held
up a book, and I could finally tell her, "Yes. This is a
true story. Her name really was Laura, and she really
lived in a little house in a big wood."

I feel the same way about faith as I listen to Luke
begin his Gospel. In no uncertain terms, he tells me:
The story I am about to tell you is the true story. This
is the story worth living for.

Jesus, I open your story, seeking truth.

January 7

"For truly I tell you, if you have faith
the size of a mustard seed, you will
say to this mountain, 'Move from
here to there,' and it will move; and
nothing will be impossible for you."

—MATTHEW 17:20

My oldest son once quit a job, which was okay since he hadn't had a raise in two years. The problem was, he didn't make sure he had another job before he left the first one.

"But Mom," he protested to my protestations, "you always say it's good to take risks."

Jesus tells us that if our faith is but the size of a mustard seed, great things can happen. It's not a call to take irrational risks but to listen to God's voice, discern the truth he's telling us, and follow, no matter how risky it may seem. It can be hard to tell the difference at times; but keeping the Lord, rather than our egos, fears, or needs, at the center of our response keeps us on course.

Jesus, nourish the seed of faith you have planted within me, and strengthen me to step forward in trust.

January 8

"For a while he refused; but later he said to himself, 'Though I have no fear of God and no respect for anyone, yet because this widow keeps bothering me, I will grant her justice, so that she may not wear me out by continually coming.'"

—LUKE 18:4–5

Ah, the fruit of persistence.

The judge in Jesus' parable has been worn down by a very bold woman, indeed. She goes before the judge herself, in a culture in which a woman would normally have a male relative speak for her. And she doesn't give up until the arrogant judge, who says he doesn't even fear God, relents.

Jesus isn't saying that God needs to be pestered into hearing our prayers. He's giving us the widow as an example of fearlessness. No matter what our need, he says, we should never be afraid to bring it before God.

Loving God, I come to you with my every need, no matter how small it seems.

January 9

In those days Jesus came from Nazareth of
Galilee and was baptized by John in the
Jordan. And just as he was coming up out of
the water, he saw the heavens torn apart
and the Spirit descending like a dove on him.
And a voice came from heaven, "You are my
Son, the Beloved; with you I am well pleased."

—MARK 1:9–11

Most of us have at least one baptism story up our
sleeves. We remember babies crying, being
startled, or just wondering about the oil and the water,
the strange fingers marking them with crosses. It was
that last moment that invariably got my children
going, by the way.

At the root, though, every baptism story is a story
about a beginning. It's the beginning of our life in
Christ, the beginning of our journey with Jesus, the
beloved Son of God.

*Jesus, help me grow in the graces I received
in my baptism.*

January 10

Now after John was arrested, Jesus came to Galilee,
proclaiming the good news of God, and saying,
"The time is fulfilled, and the kingdom of God has
come near; repent, and believe in the good news."

—MARK: 1:14–15

Who—or what—is in charge of your life?
When Jesus speaks, as he often does, of the
kingdom of God, he's talking about God's reign: over
the whole earth and in each of our lives. He's talking
about letting God be our standard and our judge, and
not allowing anything or anyone else to be in charge
of our choices, our self-understanding, or our view
of the world.

Repentance is the other word today. What false
and useless allegiances do I need to repent of? What
worldly standards and voices need to be tossed so I
can make room for God's rule in my heart?

*Loving God, I turn to you alone as my strength and
my guide.*

January 11

When they had brought their boats to shore,
they left everything and followed him.

—LUKE 5:11

For many years, I taught religion in Catholic high
schools. As you can imagine, plenty of class time
was devoted to moral issues.

Torn between a world that told students to live
one way and not worry about it, and a faith tradition
that told them that the world's way would give them
plenty to worry about, the students often asked of the
call to discipleship "Why?"

You could give lots of complicated answers to
that question, and believe me, I often did. But then
one day, I ditched the high concepts, turned to them,
and just said, "Why not?"

Jesus is calling. Jesus wants us to follow. Why not?

*Lord Jesus, give me the courage to step forward in
faith and follow you.*

January 12

That evening, at sundown, they brought to him
all who were sick or possessed with demons.

—MARK 1:32

I've been hacking and coughing for a couple of weeks now, and my husband is after me to go to the doctor. "Oh no," I say. "I'll be fine."

My older sons, away at college, are regularly afflicted with those run-down college-student colds. I tell them to go to the clinic. "No time," they say. "I'll be fine."

Why do we do this? Is it pride? Is it some misplaced sense of self-sufficiency? If the means of healing are right here, why do we turn away?

Most of us walk around harboring different kinds of pain and sickness of soul and body. Are we hiding them, hoping they'll just go away? Or can we put our pride and fear aside, lay those hurts at the feet of Jesus, and let him touch us, heal us, and make us whole?

Loving Jesus, I give you my pain and hurt, trusting in your healing touch.

January 13

They got up, drove him out of the town, and led him
to the brow of the hill on which their town
was built, so that they might hurl him off the cliff.

—LUKE 4:29

Growing up, I heard a lot about Jesus in Catholic school. We talked about his teachings on love and forgiveness. We made collages about the Beatitudes and sang songs about peace. We learned a lot of good, very true things.

Which somehow left us unprepared for passages like today's. Luke tells us that at the beginning of his ministry, Jesus preached at the Nazareth synagogue. At first, his fellow townspeople are amazed and speak "highly" of him. But then, only a few verses later, they are running him out of town and hoping to throw him off the top of a hill.

How? Why? People don't generally try to grievously hurt gentle teachers who speak about love. Perhaps there is more to Jesus than I thought. Perhaps I should listen and let Jesus surprise me.

Jesus, open my eyes and heart to all that you are.

January 14

Seek the LORD while he may be found,
call upon him while he is near.
—ISAIAH 55:6

The world today is full of seekers.

To be honest, I would probably still be seeking were it not for Jesus. Thinking about God in the abstract gets me nowhere. There is both too much to think about and not enough, and hardly anything firm and solid to grasp, at least for me.

Where is God found? In Jesus.

And this is nothing but a gift. Wondering what God is like? Seeking him? Look to Jesus. Wondering what life after death holds? Look to Jesus. Seeking a sure, undeniable contact with the love of God? Seek no further: Jesus is present in Eucharist, in reconciliation—in all of word and sacrament. As a gift.

*Loving God, when I seek, turn my steps
toward Christ.*

January 15

"And no one puts new wine into old wineskins;
otherwise, the wine will burst the skins, and
the wine is lost, and so are the skins; but one
puts new wine into fresh wineskins."

—MARK 2:22

With computers these days, you can't put the newest software into an old machine, or else the whole thing just shuts down.

It could happen, too, in my spiritual life. If today I decide to incorporate some new spiritual practice into my days—more daily Mass, the rosary, more Scripture reading, meditation—but everything else remains exactly the same, it might not go well.

If I commit to pray more, even as I ignore my destructive habits and sins, I'm trying to pour new wine into an old skin. I hope that in time, one might affect the other, that my increased prayer will open my eyes and heart to what I need to change in my life; but in order for that to happen, I need to be ready to get not just new wine but a new wineskin as well.

Lord, give me the courage to let go of old, destructive parts of my life.

"Whoever is faithful in a very little is faithful also in much; and whoever is dishonest in a very little is dishonest also in much."

—LUKE 16:10

I remember when my daughter told her first lie. She was about two, and I walked into the living room to see black marker scribbles all over the front of my desk.

"Who did this?" I asked.

Without skipping a beat, little Katie said, "Chris"— her older brother. Only two years old. Can you believe it?

So with a sad, resigned sigh, I started the task of teaching honesty in this slight matter to this very little girl.

Jesus reminds me of the importance of small things today. We start small when we teach the virtues to children. The same truth applies to us, no matter how we've grown. Our small steps in faithfulness strengthen us for the long journey we are traveling.

Loving God, be with me as I discern your will, in matters large and small.

January 17

St. Anthony

Therefore take up the whole armor of God, so that
you may be able to withstand on that evil day, and
having done everything, to stand firm.

—Ephesians 6:13

Back in the third century, a man went out into the Egyptian desert to fight. His armor? Nothing but prayer.

St. Anthony embraced a life of asceticism, not for its own sake but to become more like Christ. Out there alone, with only the most negligible food, clothing, and shelter, he was indeed besieged—the stories that have come down to us are full of vivid demons doing all they can to tempt him from his call. But, armed with God's strength, he won his battle.

What's my armor? Is it God—or do I think something else can protect me?

Lord God, strengthen me today, so that I may stand firm in your truth and love.

January 18

We declare to you what was from the beginning,
what we have heard, what we have seen with
our eyes, what we have looked at and touched
with our hands.

—1 JOHN 1:1

I glanced through the big window that faced the backyard, looking for my daughter in the twilight. It didn't take long to find her. Katie lay flat on her back on top of a blanket of snow, motionless but for her hands, which she was moving slowly in front of her face, entranced it seemed, by the contrast of the white flakes falling lightly on her maroon gloves.

It was the first time she'd seen snow. She'd intended to make a snow angel, but the wonder of it all—perfect, white crystals softly falling from the sky—got the best of her, and for that moment at least, all she could do was lie in it.

God is like that. We can know about him, read about him, and even think abstract thoughts about him. But do we know how close he really is, that he is waiting for us to stretch out, be surrounded, and wonder at the touch of his love?

Heavenly Father, I open my heart to your presence.

January 19

Make me to know your ways, O LORD;
teach me your paths.
—PSALM 25:4

I adore the Internet. As a confirmed library rat, the reality of having so much information literally at my fingertips makes me almost giddy at times.

But lately, years into the Internet revolution, with scores of television channels blasting news at me around the clock, with megabookstores offering me any volume I could ever want, I'm starting to wonder:

Do I really know anything?

In the rush to get more and more information, where has wisdom gone? I sometimes think I would be better off if, instead of having hundreds of sources grabbing my attention for minutes at a time, I had only one book to contemplate all day, all week, all month.

In the din, am I able to hear God as he speaks?

Lord, in the silence, I listen to your voice.

January 20

There is no fear in love, but
perfect love casts out fear.

—1 JOHN 4:18

L ove may drive out fear, but some of us have to
take John's challenge from the other direction
first. We have to stop being afraid in order to make
room for love.

Think of how fear paralyzes us. We can say the
words "I love you," but what are those words about if,
as we say them, we harbor fearful thoughts: "Does he
really love me?" "If I let my true self come out, surely
he won't love me." "Is this going to last?"

How can love flourish, hemmed in by doubts
and fears?

Our love for God might be exactly the same.
Loving faith—handing our lives over to God in complete trust—can't happen when we fearfully hold back
part of ourselves. We might fear punishment, or we
might fear the way a God-centered life will change us.
Either way, it's fear, and it drives out perfect love.

Can we love fearlessly?

*Lord, I put my fears aside today and open my heart
to you in trust.*

January 21

And looking at those who sat around him,
he said, "Here are my mother and my
brothers! Whoever does the will of God is
my brother and sister and mother."

—MARK 3:34–35

❧

I once asked the mother of a couple of students of
mine who seemed particularly well adjusted what
her secret was.

She said, "I think it might be because I've raised
them knowing that they don't belong to me. I see them
as my brothers in Christ, not just my sons."

In the many years since, I've thought about this
woman's words quite often. Our children are not our
possessions, the objects of our control, and neither are
any of our other relations. Each of them are beloved of
God and are on their own journey to God, with God.

I may have parents, children, a spouse, and
friends. But the foundation of these relationships is
our bond in Christ.

❧

*Jesus, help me love others as you do—as brothers
and sisters dear to your heart.*

January 22

Can a woman forget her nursing child, or show
no compassion for the child of her womb? Even
these may forget, yet I will not forget you. See, I
have inscribed you on the palms of my hands.

—ISAIAH 49:15–16

We have an ultrasound image of one of our
sons, taken when he was about five months in
the womb. His face can be seen very clearly, and it's
exactly the same face that pops out of bed now, three
years later, demanding pancakes and "shar-shage" for
breakfast.

What's most astonishing about the image, though,
is the way the folds of the womb envelop and wrap
around this tiny one. The shadows and curves give the
distinct impression that this little boy is being nestled
in the palm of a hand.

So have we all been nestled—since conception
and even before, as the psalmist sings in Psalm 139.
No human being is an accident or unwanted, for every
human being is formed by God, loved and treasured,
our names written lovingly on the palm of his hand.

Creator God, thank you for the gift of life.

January 23

He began to teach them many things in
parables, and in his teaching he said to them:
"Listen! A sower went out to sow."

—MARK 4:2–3

❧

Here is where Jesus' preaching begins—with
parables. And this parable of seeds and soil is
the first one he tells.

I'm wondering about the soil of my own heart. I'd
like to think it's fertile and receptive, but is it?

And do I really want it to be?

❧

Lord, dispel my fear of being truly open to your word.

January 24

Let me hear what God the LORD will
speak, for he will speak peace to his
people, to his faithful, to those who
turn to him in their hearts.

—PSALM 85:8

A long while back, I was at a particularly unhappy
place in my life. I was at Mass, presenting all this
before God, feeling as if I was living in a cave with a
closed-off entrance and no exit.

Then, as I rose to go to communion, a voice
flashed through my consciousness, clearly not my
own. "I understand."

That was it. No easy solutions, no road map. Just
"I understand."

As I received him in Eucharist, I knew this
was enough.

Loving Father, I rest in your understanding presence.

CONVERSION OF ST. PAUL

Now as he was going along and approaching
Damascus, suddenly a light from heaven
flashed around him. He fell to the ground
and heard a voice saying to him, "Saul,
Saul, why do you persecute me?"

—ACTS 9:3–4

Not yet knocked from a horse, I've been converted nonetheless.

In getting my attention and turning my heart, God has used my children more often than not. I started having them early, and for that I am grateful. Through their dependence, I was converted to love as the most important way to spend my time on earth. Through their independence, I was converted to respect for God's workings in the uniqueness of every human heart.

Lord, thank you for the moments of conversion in my life.

January 26

Those who had seen what had happened to the demoniac and to the swine reported it. Then they began to beg Jesus to leave their neighborhood.

—MARK 5:16-17

This story never fails to startle me at some level. Jesus has just driven out unclean spirits from a man who lived among the tombs in his torment. Jesus drove the spirits into pigs, which have run off a cliff. The townspeople hear of it and arrive to find the formerly possessed man in his right mind, quietly sitting.

Then the townspeople turn and beg Jesus to leave.

How strange. Who wouldn't prefer life to death? Who could witness the power of God and then turn from it, begging for life to go back to normal?

Who?

Jesus, open my heart to the fullness of life.

You know no God but me,
and besides me there is no savior.
—HOSEA 13:4

A little loyalty can go a long way, I've discovered. He is about three years old, and still, my little son will have only me for comfort. When he's frightened or hurt, there can be a dozen other people in the room, all related to him, all of whom have been the objects of his affection, but only I will do for holding, comforting, and wiping away tears.

It's flattering, but forgive me if at times—like in the middle of preparing dinner or when I'm about to step into the shower—someone else would do.

I wonder. Do I have the same attitude toward God as my son has toward me? When I am hurt or seeking meaning, do I always think of going to God first?

Loving Father, I give you what hurts, knowing you will comfort me.

January 28

St. Thomas Aquinas

Therefore I prayed, and understanding was given me;
I called on God, and the spirit of wisdom came to me.
—Wisdom 7:7

I grew up a faculty brat, on various college campuses. I have known many people with many degrees. All are smart, but only some have been wise.

In the midst of writing his *Summa Theologiae*, St. Thomas Aquinas had a mystical experience during Mass. He never finished the works and said, "All that I have written seems to me like straw compared to what has been revealed to me."

We've been given rational minds by God, to be used, obviously. But it's worth considering: Are my smarts getting in the way of my wisdom?

Seat of wisdom, bring light to my heart.

January 29

As it is, there are many members, yet one body.
The eye cannot say to the hand, "I have no need
of you," nor again the head to the feet, "I have no
need of you." On the contrary, the members of the
body that seem to be weaker are indispensable.

—1 CORINTHIANS 12:20–22

One Sunday, my teenaged son sat along with the
rest of us in the pew, waiting for the collection
basket to come our way.

The usher thrust the basket down our pew, past
all the adults, then snatched it back before it even
reached my son, who was practically waving his dollar bills in the air.

The usher, I suppose, couldn't imagine that a
teenager could have anything to offer.

*Lord, teach me to value the gifts of all those who
work to build your kingdom.*

January 30

"Do not store up for yourselves treasures
on earth, where moth and rust consume
and where thieves break in and steal."

—MATTHEW 6:19

A few years ago, we went to Graceland and, among other things, saw Elvis Presley's grave, a heavily decorated monument marking the spot.

That same summer, we also happened to visit some other graves (not that we're morbid or anything). We had difficulty finding every one of them because their markers were indistinguishable from the other flat stones surrounding them: the great Catholic writers Flannery O'Connor in Georgia and Walker Percy in Louisiana, and then in Kentucky, Thomas Merton, buried, among the other monks, under his monastic name, Fr. Louis.

The contrast was startling, in death, as it was in life. Where is your treasure? And what does it buy?

*Lord, help me discern where my treasure and
my heart lie.*

He said to them, "Come away to a deserted
place all by yourselves and rest a while."

—MARK 6:31

One of my teenaged sons was observing his
baby brother, who was fussing, as babies sometimes do.

"What's wrong with him?" he asked.

"He's tired," I answered.

"Then why doesn't he just go to sleep?" my son
inquired, consistent with his always logical frame
of mind.

When I'm frazzled, rushing, and worried, Jesus is
here. Why don't I just relax and rest in him?

Jesus, I give you my struggles and my tensions.
Help me rest in you.

February 1

> [Love] bears all things, believes all things,
> hopes all things, endures all things.
>
> —1 Corinthians 13:7

A few years ago, one of my sons was around twelve years old and in love with an unattainable angel.

One night, just as I had finished making some purchases in a store, I turned to see him furtively buying something of his own. Under protest, he showed it to me. It was a small pin. An angel.

I wanted to take it from him, because I knew he was setting himself up for disappointment. But then I remembered what his teacher had said to us parents a few weeks before: "Your children might fall in love for the first time this year. Don't brush it off. It's important, because it's the first time they'll think beyond themselves, and see another person as God sees them—with love."

So, accepting that I had to let him learn all that love is—the joy, the hope, and even the endurance of pain—I handed the pin back to him.

Loving God, give me the grace to love, even through pain.

February 2

PRESENTATION OF THE LORD

"My eyes have seen your salvation,
which you have prepared in the presence of all
peoples, a light for revelation to the Gentiles
and for glory to your people Israel."

—LUKE 2:30–32

It was a hot night in August, and we were in Cleveland, in the dark.

Having traveled across Ohio for one last, brief summer jaunt—baseball, the zoo, museums—we found ourselves in a relatively strange city in the midst of one of the most extensive blackouts the eastern United States had ever seen.

Stuck in a hotel room in a darkened city, what we would have done for just a tiny bit of light! Anything to help us make our way around those unfamiliar corners.

Simeon recognized Jesus as the light to the nations, the one for whom a darkened world—and each one of us in our own stumbling and groping—yearns.

Jesus, I give you the dark corners of my life.
Shine your light.

February 3

Taking the five loaves and the two fish, he
looked up to heaven, and blessed and broke the
loaves, and gave them to his disciples to set
before the people; and he divided the two fish
among them all. And all ate and were filled.

—MARK 6:41–42

My husband sometimes wonders why I fret so
much over meals. Why do I insist on doing so
much from scratch? Why am I insulted by his sug-
gestion that opening cans and throwing the contents
together would be just as good, and less trouble?

Because, for me, cooking isn't just a practical task.
It's symbolic. Creating meals to nourish my family is a
gift of self and an act of love.

When I approach Jesus in Eucharist, I am astonished. For here, with his own life, he nourishes me in
love, until I am satisfied.

*Lord, thank you for the gift of yourself you offer in
the eucharistic meal.*

February 4

"Even though you intended to do harm to me,
God intended it for good, in order to preserve
a numerous people, as he is doing today."

—Genesis 50:20

Thus ends the story of Joseph, who was sold into slavery by his brothers. The harm they intended him was turned, by God, into a great good as the people of both Egypt and Israel were rescued from famine by Joseph's gifts.

God's ways among us are mysterious, but one thing we do know is that turning misfortune or weakness into good is just what he does. I've seen it countless times in my own life, and there are probably just as many times I haven't because I wasn't looking.

Loving God, today I'll pay attention to what you have to show me about the painful parts of my life.

"So if the Son makes you free,
you will be free indeed."

—JOHN 8:36

I was in a ritzy department store (there was a sale) waiting to make a purchase. The woman ahead of me was talking to the clerk about her toddler daughter, whom they had declared to be "all girl." The mother went on about how much the little girl loved clothes, doing her hair, wearing baubles and bangles, and so on. This mother then signed her credit-card slip for more than three hundred dollars' worth of stuff for the little girl.

I had to wonder how free the little girl really was to form her own sense of whatever she was "all" of.

And what about me? How free am I? Do I really believe that in Christ I am free, and that no other judgments matter?

Lord, give me the courage to claim the freedom you give me to be myself.

February 6

St. Paul Miki and Companions

I have been crucified with Christ; and it is no longer
I who live, but it is Christ who lives in me.

—GALATIANS 2:19–20

The age of martyrdom is certainly not over. The
chain of Christian martyrs that began with
St. Stephen and includes St. Paul Miki and his companions continues in countless places around the
world where the practice of faith is either severely
constricted or simply banned.

When I taught high school, not many of my religion students saw much value in martyrdom. They
could not see the harm in saving your physical life by
saying a few words, as long as you continued to believe
the truth in your heart.

They saw a little better, however, when they were
asked to think about the alternative: a church without
martyrs. What would that be like? After all, if a truth
isn't worth dying for, how can it be worth living for?

*Father, I pray for those persecuted for their faith
around the world today.*

February 7

O LORD, you have searched me and known me.

—PSALM 139:1

Distractions during prayer can be hard to deal with. Our instinct is to push them away because they're interfering.

Sometimes distractions truly can be idle, but other times they're not. We forget that God knows us completely and wants us completely. If concerns about a child, a relationship, or another personal issue insist on entering our thoughts during prayer, perhaps that is not a distraction at all.

Perhaps that is what we're supposed to be praying about.

Lord, I present my whole life to you today in my prayer.

February 8

So make up your minds not to prepare your
defense in advance; for I will give you words
and a wisdom that none of your opponents
will be able to withstand or contradict.

—LUKE 21:14–15

If you're like me, you often think of just the right
thing to say in a conversation—two hours later.
This can be especially true of conversations about
faith, even more so when we're put on the defensive.
So it's natural to try to prevent being tongue-tied by
studying Scripture, theology, and apologetics. There's
nothing wrong with that. We should be able to give
accurate answers when we're asked about our faith.

But perhaps there is more to it. In speaking to his
disciples about persecution, Jesus actually tells them
not to prepare a defense but to trust in the wisdom he
will give that will be inarguable.

What might that irrefutable testimony be? Perhaps
St. Francis has the answer: "Go out and preach the
Gospel. Use words, if necessary."

*Jesus, help me live in a way that witnesses to the
power of your love.*

February 9

"If any of you put a stumbling block before
one of these little ones who believe in me, it
would be better for you if a great millstone
were fastened around your neck and you
were drowned in the depth of the sea."

—MATTHEW 18:6

It happens every time. We have a little one running around the house, and the older siblings insist, no matter how many times they've been warned, on "helping" the toddler walk.

What happens? You guessed it. The toddler's balance is upset by the helping hand, and down she goes.

There are many ways we can be stumbling blocks in another's path. Sometimes we do so even by trying to help. Inadvertently, we stifle independence, we cut off conversation, or we miss the point because we can't imagine that anyone can do without our insight, and we simply forget to listen.

Lord, teach me to listen to others' hearts and help in a way that really helps.

February 10

Observe the sabbath day and keep it holy,
as the LORD your God commanded you.
—DEUTERONOMY 5:12

I was once invited to give a talk on the importance of keeping Sunday holy, as a day of rest.

My husband laughed. He was right to laugh, for like many, I had fallen into the trap of seeing Sunday as a day to work on things I didn't have time for during the rest of the week.

But as I was reminded then—and am again right now—embracing rest on the Sabbath isn't an option. It's a command. That's enough to make one stop and think, isn't it?

Lord, this Sunday, remind me to rest and trust that the world is in your hands.

February 11

OUR LADY OF LOURDES

"O daughter, you are blessed by the Most High
God above all other women on earth."
—JUDITH 13:18

When the poor, sickly peasant girl Bernadette saw
an apparition of Mary in a grotto in Lourdes,
France, she described the figure she saw as a *jeune
fille*—a "young girl" of about her own height.

Her own testimony, however, was most often
ignored in subsequent representations of the apparition, something that evidently annoyed Bernadette
very much.

Bernadette knew what—and who—she saw, and
she remained faithful to the gift of that experience in
every way.

Holy Mary, mother of God, pray for us.

February 12

Let me hear of your steadfast love in the morning,
for in you I put my trust.
Teach me the way I should go,
for to you I lift up my soul.

—PSALM 143:8

What are my early morning hopes as I look to a new day? What will make this a good day for me? A successful meeting? No family fights? Getting the lawn work or laundry done? What will satisfy me?

Or is growing in God's love enough to make it a great day, today and always?

Lord, focus me on your will for me in whatever I do today.

February 13

After this he went out and saw a tax collector named Levi, sitting at the tax booth; and he said to him, "Follow me." And he got up, left everything, and followed him.

—LUKE 5:27–28

A second chance—just imagine what you would do with a second chance if it were offered to you. It is.

Jesus, take this part of my life. Thank you for a second chance.

February 14

Rejoice with Jerusalem, and be glad for her,
all you who love her;
rejoice with her in joy,
all you who mourn over her—
that you may nurse and be satisfied
from her consoling breast;
that you may drink deeply with delight
from her glorious bosom.

—ISAIAH 66:10–11

When I wander around art museums, I'm always glad to see paintings representing the virtue of charity, for it is invariably symbolized, as it has been since ancient times, by a mother nursing children. In charity, we give of ourselves in love, and that is just what we do when we nurse. We give of our own bodies so that another person can live and thrive.

No matter if we have nursed children or not, we know this, and we have lived it in different ways. We know that love is nothing but a joyous round of giving: from God to us, then through us to others, and back again. Abundantly and with delight.

Loving God, be with me today as I share the love you have given me.

February 15

No one after lighting a lamp puts it under
the bushel basket, but on the lampstand,
and it gives light to all in the house.

—MATTHEW 5:15

✣

We were attending Mass at a Byzantine Rite Catholic Church one evening. It was the vigil of a feast, the power was out, it was hot and dark, and the congregation was very small—about fifteen people.

About ten minutes into the liturgy, as the priest was chanting his way up to and around the altar, a voice rose from the congregation.

"Wait a minute, Father," an older woman yelled, and she continued speaking in a very loud tone to another woman, who had lost her place in the prayer book. This went on for about a minute, the priest and the rest of us frozen in place as the instruction continued.

An odd example, perhaps, of light shining in darkness, but I'll stick by it. May I be as undeterred as this woman when I am challenged daily to reach out to others.

✣

Loving God, give me the courage to share the light of your love today.

February 16

But when Simon Peter saw it, he fell down
at Jesus' knees, saying, "Go away from me,
Lord, for I am a sinful man!"
—LUKE 5:8

Many years ago when I was teaching high school, one of my students disappeared. For weeks and weeks she wasn't in class. Her parents told the administration that she was sick or away or something, and we were told to just keep marking her absent.

Then one day, she reappeared, smiling, as if she'd not been gone at all. And then a couple of months after her return she shyly brought out baby pictures.

Why was the family so secretive about this? I don't know, and I can't judge. But I do know that what this experience symbolized to me was our rush to shut ourselves off when we have sinned or failed. In shame, we remove ourselves from the presence of others, and, worst of all, from God.

Lord, I have sinned. I have failed. Help me to live in your mercy rather than in shame.

February 17

Do not neglect to show hospitality to strangers,
for by doing that some have entertained angels
without knowing it.

—HEBREWS 13:2

In my midsize Midwestern town, there is a large Burmese community, which happens to include a small group of Buddhist monks. Their *wat,* or monastery, is about a mile from my house, and I see the monks all the time. I see them at the post office and the grocery store most of all. They are usually buying rice and root vegetables, but last week two of them, bald and in their flowing, burnished-orange robes, were doing some serious shopping in the greeting-card aisle.

I would love to start up a conversation with them, but I have no idea what to say. I hope that someday I'll be brave enough.

Loving God, help me to see you in a stranger today.

February 18

So, whether you eat or drink, or whatever you do,
do everything for the glory of God.

—1 CORINTHIANS 10:31

If I really were to do everything for God's glory
today, what would change?

It's a lot like changing diapers. You can see it in
its starkest, most mechanical terms, or you can see it
as an act of love. Then somehow, what was a burden
becomes a privilege.

Working for God's glory today may not change
what I do as much as it changes how I do it.

Lord, I give my day to you, for your glory.

February 19

Then he looked up at his disciples and said:
"Blessed are you who are poor,
for yours is the kingdom of God."

—LUKE 6:20

One summer, I did volunteer work in a rural part of Kentucky. The area was terribly poor, but the local Catholic parish was made up primarily of professional people. Most of the poor people we visited and the children who came to our Bible school didn't belong to the parish.

One Sunday, though, an elderly farm couple showed up at Mass. They were dressed shabbily, and they smelled rather bad. Many in the congregation were not pleased, and there was conversation after Mass to the effect that someone should tell them to clean up or not return.

As far as I know, the couple never came back.

Jesus, move me to real solidarity with the lives of the poor.

February 20

The human mind plans the way,
but the LORD directs the steps.
—PROVERBS 16:9

I had the evening all planned out: nice, home-cooked meal; piano practicing; plenty of time to do homework; bed.

That is until, on the way home, my eldest son cautiously told me that there was a basketball game in the evening that he'd forgotten about. That is until we arrived home to find many new baby hamsters, lots of whom had been half-consumed by their mother, necessitating intense grief counseling. That is until . . . So much for my plans. The present moment calls.

Lord, help me be mindful of your call to serve every moment today, no matter what happens.

At once the man was made well, and he took
up his mat and began to walk. Now that day
was a sabbath. So the Jews said to the man
who had been cured, "It is the sabbath; it is
not lawful for you to carry your mat."

—JOHN 5:9–10

The fellow hadn't been able to walk for almost forty years, Jesus heals him, and the first response of witnesses is to scold him for carrying his mat on the Sabbath.

Talk about missing the point.

When we go to Mass, we can sometimes find it challenging not to play the role of a critic. My downfall is the music and the homily. Others find it irresistible to criticize what others are wearing or who's going to communion or whose children are misbehaving.

As I said, talk about missing the point.

*Lord Jesus, help me focus on your loving presence
and mighty deeds.*

February 22

Jesus said to them, ". . . Do you still not perceive
or understand? Are your hearts hardened? Do
you have eyes, and fail to see? Do you have ears,
and fail to hear? And do you not remember?"

—MARK 8:17–18

On the highest hill in Montreal stands St. Joseph's
Oratory, built at the inspiration and prayer of
Blessed Andre Bessette. One of the relics of Blessed
Andre on display is his heart, encased in a reddish glass
container. Standing, as one must, at some distance
from this relic, I peered, looking for it. I couldn't see
anything. My husband kept saying, "There it is—see?"
But I never could discern its shape.

Throughout his Gospel, Mark highlights the spiritual blindness of the disciples, as he does in today's
reading. As the Gospel proceeds, it's clear that this is
because they have not suffered yet, so they have not
yet trodden the path of the real disciple.

My faith tells me that God is never absent. But
sometimes, for many reasons, I just can't see.

Lord, give me eyes to see and ears to hear.

St. Polycarp

Formerly, when you did not know God, you were
enslaved to beings that by nature are not gods.
Now, however, that you have come to know God, or
rather to be known by God, how can you turn back
again to the weak and beggarly elemental spirits?
How can you want to be enslaved to them again?

—Galatians 4:8–9

The story told is that as the elderly bishop
St. Polycarp was presented to the crowds at
the arena, he was instructed to deny his faith by
pronouncing "Away with the atheists!"—meaning
the Christians, whom the Romans considered
nonbelievers.

So Polycarp complied. Motioning to the massive
crowd gathered to see him burned, he waved his hand,
looked to heaven, and said, "Away with the atheists."

My culture still worships many gods. Do I stand in
relation to those gods as an atheist—or as a believer?

God, you are the only Lord of my life.

February 24

You must understand this, my beloved:
let everyone be quick to listen, slow to
speak, slow to anger; for your anger
does not produce God's righteousness.

—JAMES 1:19–20

Our anger can be righteous. But often, it is not. If I want to know when I've gone too far, I find one measure that's never wrong. It's the look of complete bewilderment in the other person's eyes when confronted with my anger.

That's as powerful a reminder as I need to be quiet and remember who is God—and who isn't.

Lord, calm any anger in my heart, and help me trust you more.

February 25

Jesus went on with his disciples to the villages
of Caesarea Philippi; and on the way he asked
his disciples, "Who do people say that I am?"

—MARK 8:27

Who is Jesus? If we look around, we see lots of
different variations on the theme of Jesus. Lots
of opinions.

I often find that the more intense and wild the
speculation, the less interest the speculator has in the
most reliable sources we have when it comes to the
question of who Jesus is: the Scriptures and the life of
his church.

Who do I say that he is? Am I just curious—or
does the answer really matter? Where do I go to get to
know the One who loves me so?

*Jesus, may I know who you are as I meet you in word
and sacrament.*

February 26

Let this be recorded for a generation to come,
so that a people yet unborn may praise the LORD:
that he looked down from his holy height,
from heaven the LORD looked at the earth.

—PSALM 102:18–19

My world is very small sometimes, even though I try to think big. Too much of the time I do what I do just for the present and mostly for myself.

How the psalmist uproots me and replants me. This life isn't just about me. It's about God's plan for all of creation, and for some amazing reason, I am a part of that. We all are—so generations yet unborn may know God's love.

Creator God, bless the work of my hands for those living and those to be born.

February 27

Faithful friends are a sturdy shelter:
whoever finds one has found a treasure.

—SIRACH 6:14

God surely loves us through our friends. In their sympathy, support, patience, and loyalty, God's love shines clearly.

I hope that my friends find God's blessing in my friendship, as well.

Lord, today I thank you for my friends.

February 28

So then, putting away falsehood, let all
of us speak the truth to our neighbors,
for we are members of one another.

—EPHESIANS 4:25

What are the worst kinds of lies? I sometimes think that they're the ones made up of silence rather than words.

In fact, I can't remember the last time I outright lied using words. But I can remember the last time I remained silent when truth was called for and I was too afraid to offer it.

Jesus, you are "the way, and the truth, and the life." Fill me with your truth.

March

March 1

Blow the trumpet in Zion;
sanctify a fast.

—Joel 2:15

We might wonder—what's the point? What impact can our treatment of our bodies have on our spiritual selves?

To answer that, we need look no further than the modern incarnation of fasting: the diet. Why do we constantly and endlessly seek to lose weight? Because of our physical health, to be sure, but for most of us it's also about wanting to feel better about ourselves.

The fasting that Christians do is not about feeling better about ourselves, nor is it about losing weight. It is, however, very much about the connection between body and spirit. When I deny myself, I learn that perhaps I don't need all the things I think I need. When I don't look to things to satisfy me, I'm forced to look to God for my peace, and to wonder if all these material satisfactions are helping or hindering my journey to God.

Loving God, may my sacrifices bring me closer to you.

March 2

Jesus looked at them and said, "For mortals it is impossible, but not for God; for God all things are possible."

—MARK 10:27

The boy next door is in his backyard practicing with a soccer ball. He wears his uniform, so there must be a game today. He kicks and dribbles, balances the ball, perfecting his skills. He wants to do well. And he probably will. But he'll also probably fall short of his own expectations, and he'll fail somehow, perhaps in a way visible only to himself.

We often have the same attitude toward our spiritual lives. We want to know what to do and how to do it really well. Jesus speaks these words to a rich, young man and to his disciples, reminding us that those are the wrong questions because, in that framework of spirituality, we will always "fail."

The goal of this journey is not that we perfect ourselves but that we learn to let God do the perfecting.

Lord, help me let go and let you work in my life.

Marct 3

Who is a God like you, pardoning iniquity
and passing over the transgression
of the remnant of your possession?
He does not retain his anger forever,
because he delights in showing clemency.
—MICAH 7:18

When I was five years old, I did a terrible thing:
I swiped my friend's mother's diamond ring
right. I remember hardly anything about the crime
itself; what I remember is the moment of discovery—I
had worn the ring in the bathtub, it slipped off, and
my mother found it before it went down the drain.

I remember all that plus the guilt I felt, a feeling
that still echoes in my conscience. I remember my
mother telling me how worried this woman, a widow,
was about the loss of her—gulp—engagement ring.

Sorrow for sin is, of course, essential. But it's a
problem when guilty memories of sin overshadow the
reality of God's forgiveness. Sometimes I think that
the biggest step in faith we can make is to let mercy,
rather than guilt, guide our steps.

Lord, I'm sorry for the way I have harmed others.
Open my heart to your forgiveness.

March 4

Your Father knows what you
need before you ask him.
—MATTHEW 6:8

If you've worked in a specific field for any length of time, you know that there are only so many questions you're going to be asked.

Schoolteachers improve with age because they can anticipate problems students will have with material. The more experience a supervisor has, the greater help he or she can be to new employees.

It's not magic. It's understanding that grows from wisdom and love, the same wisdom and love—on a much smaller scale, of course—that God has for us, his own students, his own children.

Lord, today I come to you with my greatest needs, in confidence and trust.

March 5

When Jesus saw him lying there and knew
that he had been there a long time, he said
to him, "Do you want to be made well?"

—JOHN 5:6

The question Jesus asks seems strange. Of course,
we think. Why bother asking? Who wouldn't
rather be healthy than sick?

Well, when I think about my own life, I can think
of plenty of times I've harbored a kind of soul sickness. I've nurtured anger and envy and resentment. At
any time, I could have let go of them, but sometimes it
took a long time. What was I afraid of?

Jesus asks me again today, "Do you want to
be well?"

Jesus, I want to be well. Heal me.

Remember these things, O Jacob,
and Israel, for you are my servant;
I formed you, you are my servant;
O Israel, you will not be forgotten by me.
—ISAIAH 44:21

I don't know how the parents of really large families cope emotionally. I've got only five children, and they've just about worn out my worry beads. I could literally sit all day and worry about them. But instead of worrying, I try to pray.

God won't give up on any worrisome child whom he has formed. I can take comfort and strength from that as a parent—and, come to think of it, as a child, as well.

Lord, I place my family in your care.

"Ask, and it will be given you; search, and you will find; knock, and the door will be opened for you."
—MATTHEW 7:7

For years, my oldest son and I had a running joke. He'd say to me, out of the blue, "Can I have a dollar?" I'd always say no. The joke, I suppose, was ultimately about my stinginess. Of course, I wouldn't just give him a dollar for no reason. That wouldn't be like me.

One night, we came out of the movies. He asked. I whipped out a bill and handed it to him. He stood stunned and then laughed. Now this was really funny. After all these years, he finally got his dollar.

We, too, might be surprised by God's unexpected answers to our prayers.

Loving God, I trust in your response to my prayers.

This is right and is acceptable in the sight of God
our Savior, who desires everyone to be saved and to
come to the knowledge of the truth.

—1 TIMOTHY 2:3–4

Looking down on the earth from the window of an
airplane, I can't help but be awed and humbled by
the fact that each one of the thousands of homes in my
sight contains a story—as many intricate, painful, and
joyful stories as there are people inside.

And God created each one of these people
who are living out the stories of their lives, created
them out of love. God is watching over each one, intimately involved in each life, whispering through each
conscience.

I'm reminded that I'm not the center of the universe. God's love embraces all of us. And within the
limitations of my humanity, so should mine.

*Lord, I pray for all of your children. May we journey
to you together in love.*

They said to one another, "Here comes this
dreamer. Come now, let us kill him and throw
him into one of the pits; then we shall say
that a wild animal has devoured him, and we
shall see what will become of his dreams."

—GENESIS 37:19–20

We call jealousy a green-eyed monster for a very
good reason: it destroys. Few stories express
this truth more profoundly than the story of Joseph.
We can see the destructive power of jealousy in
our own lives when we consider how it can devour
something very important: our gratitude.

Think about it. When I'm jealous, I'm saying
that what God has given me isn't good enough. So
next time I feel like saying "I wish," perhaps I will say
"thank you" instead.

*Lord, today I thank you for my life as it is, not as I
wish it would be.*

"Whoever does not carry the cross and
follow me cannot be my disciple."
—LUKE 14:27

My preteen daughter is always looking for odd
jobs to do around the house that might bring
her a little extra income. Now, that sounds great, but
we told her years ago that if she wanted an allowance,
all she had to do, for starters, was keep her own room
clean. Which has never happened. It's easier to look
elsewhere than tend to her own messes.

In today's Gospel, Jesus calls us to accept our
crosses. He doesn't tell us to go out and find new and
creative crosses or mortifications, or to find something extra to make our lives more difficult. He simply
tells us to accept the crosses that discipleship sends us,
no matter what the cost.

Jesus, strengthen me to carry my crosses in love.

March 11

As he came near and saw the city, he wept over it, saying, "If you, even you, had only recognized on this day the things that make for peace! But now they are hidden from your eyes. Indeed, the days will come upon you, when your enemies will set up ramparts around you and surround you, and hem you in on every side."

—LUKE 19:41–43

I once had a student in a high-school religion class who would not stop asking about God and suffering. As it turned out, his question emerged from the painful experience of seeing a family friend die of a protracted, painful disease. If he, as a relatively powerless teen, would have done anything to help this friend, why wouldn't the all-powerful God?

The Christian answer to suffering is best summed up not in words but in a person: Jesus. In Jesus, God suffers with us. He suffers on the cross and in today's Gospel reading, he weeps over the future pain of Jerusalem.

In our suffering, we are not alone.

Loving God, may all who suffer be aware of your comforting presence.

March 12

"Truly I tell you, whatever you bind on earth
will be bound in heaven, and whatever you
loose on earth will be loosed in heaven."
—MATTHEW 18:18

My religion students often asked when they "had to" go to confession and how often. Many of us wonder the same thing, and in so doing we reveal our view of this sacrament as an obligation.

But is it possible to see it another way? How about as a gift? For we know how our sins nag at us, eat at us, and how hard it is to believe that we've really been forgiven.

Hearing the words of forgiveness . . . we know. And we can go on in joyful hope.

Lord, thank you for the gift of your mercy.

March 13

And the Spirit immediately drove him out into
the wilderness. He was in the wilderness forty
days, tempted by Satan; and he was with the
wild beasts; and the angels waited on him.

—MARK 1:12–13

In our own deserts we, too, are tempted. My own
way through temptation is often to stand back and
view the big picture. How am I going to feel about
myself if I give in to temptation? What will I gain?
What will I lose?

I know I want to be a person of integrity who lives
by her values. Why am I so willing to let go of integrity at this moment?

Jesus, strengthen me against temptation.

Then the devil took him to Jerusalem, and placed
him on the pinnacle of the temple, saying to him,
"If you are the Son of God, throw yourself down
from here, for it is written,
'He will command his angels concerning you,
to protect you,' and
'On their hands they will bear you up,
so that you will not dash your foot against a stone.'"
Jesus answered him, "It is said, 'Do not put the
Lord your God to the test.'"

–LUKE 4:9–12

I am quite serious in saying that my worst sins have
been committed when I was convinced that I was
really close to God. Doing all of those good external
religious acts, I thought I was protected. And since
I wanted to be good, all my motivations and desires
were covered under some strange Faith Warranty. In a
way, I am doing nothing but putting God to a test.

But no. The powers that want to harm and
bring darkness never rest and are always waiting to
return—watching for the moments that I think I've
got my spiritual life covered and can do no wrong.

*Lord, root out pride from my life, and teach me to
depend on you.*

March 15

Then Peter said to Jesus,
"Lord, it is good for us to be here."
—MATTHEW 17:4

On a trip to New York City, I was glad to be able to view an exhibit of El Greco's works at the Metropolitan Museum of Art.

I'd seen plenty of El Greco in art books, but nothing prepared me for actually seeing the paintings in person: huge canvases with fluid figures reaching, churning, swirling upward toward the heavens. It was good to be there.

Knowing about something can never compare to personal experience and presence, as the disciples on the mountain with Jesus saw so clearly.

Lord, it is good to be in the presence of your love.

But the LORD was not in the fire; and after the
fire a sound of sheer silence. When Elijah
heard it, he wrapped his face in his mantle and
went out and stood at the entrance of the
cave. Then there came a voice to him that said,
"What are you doing here, Elijah?"
—1 KINGS 19:12–13

Such a noisy world we live in. Between television,
radio, and the visual riot of advertising and urban
sprawl, it's so hard to find a space that's quiet.

But as Elijah' s experience reminds me, perhaps I
should try a little harder. Who knows what good news
I might hear.

*Lord, today I still myself so that I may hear
your voice.*

March 17

But if anyone has caused pain, he has caused it not to me, but to some extent—not to exaggerate it—to all of you. This punishment by the majority is enough for such a person; so now instead you should forgive and console him, so that he may not be overwhelmed by excessive sorrow. So I urge you to reaffirm your love for him.

—2 Corinthians 2:5–8

As a parent, I am not always convinced that "excessive sorrow" for sin would be such a bad thing. I'd like to see a little excessive sorrow once in a while, to be honest.

But Paul is right, as he always is. The failure to forgive serves no purpose except a destructive one.

I always appreciate the gift of being able to begin again. Can I offer that gift to someone else?

Loving, forgiving God, help me to share your mercy with someone today.

"To what then will I compare the people of this
generation, and what are they like?
For John the Baptist has come eating no bread and
drinking no wine, and you say, 'He has a demon';
the Son of Man has come eating and drinking, and
you say, 'Look, a glutton and a drunkard, a friend
of tax collectors and sinners!'"

—LUKE 7:31, 33–34

My toddler son goes to a babysitter some mornings. He knows the routine, but still, he's a little tense on those mornings. He rarely cries outright anymore, but I can see in his eyes and quivering lip: "Don't go!"

Touching, but when I return a few hours later, he usually runs away from me yelling, "I don't wanna go home!"

Make up your mind, I think.

Sometimes we can't make up our minds about God's ways. We yearn for his presence and his intervention, but then when we actually experience him, we draw back, afraid of how we might be changed.

*Loving God, open me to your guidance in every
circumstance.*

March 19

> Brothers and sisters, do not be children in
> your thinking; rather, be infants in evil,
> but in thinking be adults.
>
> —1 CORINTHIANS 14:20

Once, when I was still teaching, I was visiting my mother, and she eyed me up and down. "So," she asked, "what do you wear to work?"

I might have been twenty-eight, but at that moment, emotionally, I was not a day over thirteen.

We all have different triggers, but there they are—the words, moments, or even glances that can wipe away years of hard-earned maturity. It can happen with our faith and its symbols, as well, if we link them with some negative past experience—shame or the hypocrisy of others.

Perhaps it is time to grow up.

Loving Father, help me grow in faith and respond to you in maturity, freed from the past.

March 20

But take care and watch yourselves closely,
so as neither to forget the things that your eyes
have seen nor to let them slip from your mind
all the days of your life; make them known to
your children and your children's children.
—DEUTERONOMY 4:9

As my daughter works her way through a piano piece, something strange often happens. The first week, she's got it and can play through the piece smoothly. But then her teacher tells her to work on the fine points of dynamics and rhythm, and suddenly the whole thing falls apart. What she could fly through yesterday is a stumbling block today. Given this new information, she has to relearn the piece. Note by note.

As we grow and age, we sometimes find that what we learned ten years ago is not so helpful today. Our faith is still strong, but new circumstances and a host of new fine points force us to explore new ways of living it. We have to relearn; at the same time, we don't forget that God is still with us, no matter how life changes. Step by step. Note by note.

Jesus, I want to follow you more closely. Teach me how to bear these new burdens.

March 21

Clear me from hidden faults.

—PSALM 19:12

Small children are usually so unceasingly active, they can wear you out quickly. So when they fall into quiet, who wouldn't be relieved?

Relieved, until you discover the crayon marks on the wall, spilled water, and an empty spool of toilet paper. You quickly learn that if they're not making noise, they're probably up to no good.

God might feel the same way about me and my spiritual silences. If I find myself in a period where I'm not praying much and I really don't want to, I can usually find the reason: There's something I'd prefer to keep hidden from God's eyes and ears.

Lord, I search my heart and present my secrets to you.

March 22

"The Pharisee, standing by himself, was praying
thus, 'God, I thank you that I am not like other
people: thieves, rogues, adulterers, or even like
this tax collector. I fast twice a week; I give a
tenth of all my income.' But the tax collector,
standing far off, would not even look up to
heaven, but was beating his breast and saying,
'God, be merciful to me, a sinner!'"

—LUKE 18:11–13

Complaints about Mass abound in some parishes.
The music is insipid or the homilies uninspired.
The parish isn't friendly enough or—to some intro-
verts—it's too friendly. Fellow worshippers aren't
dressed appropriately, or surely they aren't worthy to
go to communion.

Judging others in relation to ourselves can take a
lot of energy.

Meanwhile, Jesus waits.

Lord, be merciful to me, a sinner.

March 23

But God, who is rich in mercy, out of the
great love with which he loved us even
when we were dead through our trespasses,
made us alive together with Christ.

—EPHESIANS 2:4–5

I went to a traveling exhibit of Vatican "treasures," which included the finger bone of Pope Pius V, complete with a papal ring. The exhibit was in the basement of a museum complex, and hordes of viewers, listening intently to their audio tours, streamed past.

In the Cloisters Museum in New York, you can walk along paths and under arches that, hundreds of years ago, heard the prayers of monks and nuns.

It always saddens me to see expressions of a living faith reduced to museum exhibits.

But what about my faith? Is it an exhibit I take out to display, or is it a living relationship with the real person, Jesus Christ?

Lord Jesus, live in me.

March 24

Do not harden your hearts, as at Meribah,
as on the day at Massah in the wilderness.

—PSALM 95:8

One of my older sons just got ripped off—and
I mean massively ripped off—in an online
purchase that ended up being not a purchase at all,
but a mere transfer of funds from the United States
to Romania.

My heart aches for him, but it was his money, and
he's learned a hard lesson he will not soon forget. But
still I think, if he had only listened to me, he could
have avoided all this. Sigh.

Ah, but what of me? What pain in my life could I
have avoided if only I had listened to God and trusted
his word?

*Lord, give me the courage to listen to you and live by
your word.*

ANNUNCIATION

The angel said to her, "Do not be afraid, Mary,
for you have found favor with God. And now,
you will conceive in your womb and bear a son,
and you will name him Jesus."

—LUKE 1:30–31

There is no way I could have imagined, at the beginning of any of my pregnancies, who the child within me would turn out to be.

Oh, I had my hopes and dreams, but in more than twenty years of watching the fruit of my womb grow, I have found, without exception, that the reality of each of these people is infinitely more wonderful than anything I could have planned.

Mary could not know, either. Even the angel's words could not completely express what was to come, either the pain or the joy.

But in faith, trusting that God knows best, she said yes to whatever lay in store.

Hail Mary, full of grace, the Lord is with you!

March 26

For you were called to freedom, brothers
and sisters; only do not use your freedom
as an opportunity for self-indulgence, but
through love become slaves to one another.

—GALATIANS 5:13

Christian faith, it seems to me, is largely about
irony: the least become first, death leads to life,
and single-minded commitment leads to freedom.

My students often had a hard time understanding this because, for them, faith in God seemed to be
something that constrained freedom rather than gave
it. What they didn't understand was this: When God
is first, you are free to be yourself, as he created you.
No one else's opinions or standards matter. You are
beholden to no human person or movement or trend
or need.

You are God's. Living in that awareness gives a
freedom that is breathtaking.

*Loving God, bind my heart to you so that I may find
true freedom.*

Take delight in the LORD,
and he will give you the desires of your heart.

—PSALM 37:4

I have certainly seen children who own more toys than my little son, but believe me, he has enough.

Especially since he hardly ever plays with them. Surrounded by contraptions designed to meet his desires, he usually ignores them and embraces pots, pans, spoons, empty boxes, and delights from the junk drawer instead.

The world surrounds me, too, with baubles and toys designed to amuse and fulfill my own desires. Am I taken in by them? Or do I follow the true yearning of my heart for love and delight that will never wear out?

God, help me discern what I really yearn for.

March 28

First, I thank my God through Jesus Christ
for all of you, because your faith is proclaimed
throughout the world.

—ROMANS 1:8

It was the first day of eighth grade in a new school in a new town in a new part of the country. I sat down in Tennessee History class, and a girl behind me asked my name. I told her. Then she asked, "What church do you go to?"

Taken aback, I revealed that I was Catholic. She nodded. "You look like a Catholic," she said. We became friends, but I never did figure out what she meant when she said I looked Catholic.

But I do have a sense of what a follower of Jesus looks like in word and deed. Would the rest of the world recognize me as such, if asked?

Jesus, form me as your disciple.

March 29

"Whoever is not with me is against me, and
whoever does not gather with me scatters."

—LUKE 11:23

Wouldn't I like to believe that this isn't true? But
where, indeed, have the little compromises
taken me? Have they brought me closer to Jesus or
taken me a step further away?

Jesus, I trust that you are the way.

March 30

O the depth of the riches and wisdom and
knowledge of God! How unsearchable are
his judgments and how inscrutable his ways!
—ROMANS 11:33

When my middle son was around eleven, he
got into a fight at school. Without knowing
him, you might not understand how unexpected this
incident was. He is the definition of *mild mannered:*
bookish and generally friendly.

He couldn't—or wouldn't—explain himself then,
and never has since. I was, and still remain, mystified
at his behavior.

If human beings we know and live with can be
such mysteries to us, of course, the immortal, eternal
God can as well. Sometimes we get annoyed because
God's ways are, indeed, mysterious.

But perhaps complete, rational understanding
isn't the point. Perhaps the point is love.

*Lord, deepen my love for you and for others in the
midst of mystery.*

$\mathcal{M}arch\ 31$

I will instruct you and teach you the way
you should go;
I will counsel you with my eye upon you.
Do not be like a horse or a mule, without
understanding,
whose temper must be curbed with bit and bridle,
else it will not stay near you.

—PSALM 32:8–9

Our yard borders on that of some dog owners who installed an underground electronic fence to keep their beagles contained.

One of the dogs has learned his lesson, but the other refuses to. He crosses the boundary, and ends up running around our house yelping in pain from the shock, but still refuses to return home. Or perhaps the pain prevents him from figuring out what to do.

Maybe this is what animals need. I hope it's not what I need. I hope that I can trust and listen to the Lord, following as his disciple, without running right into the pain that will come should I leave my appointed place with him.

Jesus, open my heart to listen. Strengthen my will to follow your loving guidance.

April

April 1

When Mary came where Jesus was and saw him,
she knelt at his feet and said to him, "Lord, if you
had been here, my brother would not have died."

—JOHN 11:32

How many times have we uttered words like these?
"If only, God . . . if only. Why?"

As Mary confronts Jesus, I see that faith doesn't
mean the end of questions.

It might just mean a completely different kind of
answer, one I never would have received if I had not
asked, and if I had not asked in faith.

Heavenly Father, I give you my hardest questions.
Help me listen to your answer.

April 2

More than that, I regard everything as loss
because of the surpassing value of knowing
Christ Jesus my Lord. For his sake I have
suffered the loss of all things, and I regard them
as rubbish, in order that I may gain Christ.
—PHILIPPIANS 3:8

I have given up things that I thought stood between me and Christ, because that is what we do during this time of year.

In the process, I have, indeed, grown closer to Christ. I've found that I don't need half of what I think I need to be happy.

Am I prepared to make this a way of life, instead of just a yearly observance?

Lord, give me the strength to put what keeps me from you behind me forever.

April 3

Jesus straightened up and said to her, "Woman,
where are they? Has no one condemned you?"
She said, "No one, sir." And Jesus said, "Neither
do I condemn you. Go your way, and from now
on do not sin again."

—JOHN 8:10–11

I find this one of the most powerful moments in
all of Scripture. As many times as I have read and
heard this story, Jesus' words at the end always sound
out clearly, like a bell, as if they were being spoken
directly to me, right here and right now.

Perhaps they are.

*Jesus, help me believe and live out of the truth that
you do not condemn me.*

April 4

I will call to mind the deeds of the LORD;
I will remember your wonders of old.

—PSALM 77:11

The life of faith has its ups and downs. Sometimes it's easy to connect with God and feel his presence; other times it's not.

When it's tough and God seems far away, I often try to remember moments when I was sure, when I was caught up in the reality and possibility of God's love. Some of those moments were a long time ago: the night of my senior retreat in high school, when I sat alone in the pillow-strewn chapel of the retreat house, recognizing to the depths of my heart that I was encountering the real presence.

Sometimes the moments are closer in time, such as last Sunday at Mass or that evening recently when through the mess of everyday life an innocent child's face shone, a face born out of the love of three people— me, my husband, and an amazing God who works in such mysterious ways.

Lord, I remember the moments I have dwelt in your presence.

April 5

The simple believe everything,
but the clever consider their steps.
—PROVERBS 14:15

W hen I taught high-school religion classes, I was
always struck by a double standard among
many of my students.

They approached the Scriptures and Christian
teaching with unyielding skepticism. But some of
these same kids would rush into my classroom full
of enthusiasm for what they'd just discovered about
the predictions of Nostradamus or what their best
friend's cousin's boss told them about a haunted house
or Ouija board experience.

Well, what about me? Am I really open to the truth
of what God tells me through his word, or do I bring
a skepticism to the promise of mercy, love, and hope
that ultimately closes me off from the deepest riches
of faith?

Lord, deepen my trust in your word.

April 6

Paul, called to be an apostle of Christ Jesus
by the will of God, and our brother Sosthenes,
To the church of God that is in Corinth, to
those who are sanctified in Christ Jesus, called
to be saints, together with all those who in
every place call on the name of our Lord Jesus
Christ, both their Lord and ours.

—1 Corinthians 1:1–2

We live in a society that celebrates individualism. We're also part of a church that sometimes lets us down. So there's a great temptation to try to separate our "personal faith" from organized religion.

A simple reading of even two verses from Paul tells me that it cannot be done. God calls me to life—not all on my own, fortunately. I am part of a people, part of creation, that is God's.

I am not on this road alone. Thank God, literally, for that.

Lord, open me to the wisdom of your body, the church.

April 7

For my thoughts are not your thoughts,
nor are your ways my ways, says the LORD.
—ISAIAH 55:8

Father Solanus Casey was a member of the Capuchin order whose attempts to answer God's call were continually frustrated.

He was rejected by seminaries, or flunked out of them. He struggled through courses, and when he finally was ordained, was ordained as a priest simplex: He could say Mass, but he wasn't supposed to preach or hear confessions. Apparently, his superiors worried that his intellectual struggles indicated a decreased capacity for preaching and advising.

Today we remember Solanus Casey for something very interesting. He spent most of his life as a "porter" in his religious communities, receiving visitors at the door. In that capacity, Solanus Casey heard thousands of stories of suffering and pain, received thousands of requests for prayer, and gave countless words of compassion, hope—and wisdom.

I love to see how God will always find a way.

*Lord, help me use my gifts in whatever way
I can today.*

April 8

Be imitators of me, as I am of Christ.
—1 CORINTHIANS 11:1

I was once standing in line at the grocery store, impatient as always, hand on my hip, tapping my foot.

Looking down to my then five-year-old daughter, I couldn't help but be startled. There she stood, wearing sunglasses and holding her purse. One hand was on her hip, and she was tapping her foot. She sighed.

It was a little scary. How else was she imitating me, I wondered. Maybe I need to be a little more careful!

And who's my role model? Whose stance toward God am I imitating, consciously or not?

Jesus, guide my thoughts and actions in imitation of you and those who love you.

April 9

Then those who went ahead and those who
followed were shouting,
"Hosanna!
Blessed is the one who comes in the name
of the Lord!"

—MARK 11:9

As Jesus entered Jerusalem, crowds surrounded him, praising.

A few days later, he stood alone.

I can easily shake my head at this, wondering, *How can people be so fickle?*

Was I unyielding in my faithfulness to Jesus this week? Did I stand firm in love, no matter what the cost?

Jesus, strengthen me to greater faithfulness to you in matters great and small.

April 10

Simon Peter said to him, "Lord, where are you going?" Jesus answered, "Where I am going, you cannot follow me now; but you will follow afterward."

—JOHN 13:36

At that final meal, Jesus seems to be putting a distance between himself and his friends. What he will suffer, he will suffer alone.

But faith reveals another, almost ironic dimension to this tragic picture: His lonely sufferings ultimately bring our own seemingly endless loneliness to an end. Through Jesus' acceptance of the dark abandonment that evil seeks to impose on creation, the power of that force is shattered, and wholeness is possible.

Right now, the distance is great, and we cannot follow. But Jesus assures us that the journey will be ours someday, as well, and because he took it first, it will end in joy.

Jesus, we stand as humble and grateful witnesses to your sacrifice of love.

April 11

God raised the Lord and will
also raise us by his power.

—1 Corinthians 6:14

Several years ago, I gave birth to a little boy.
Just a few days later, on today's date, my own mother
passed away. She was buried during Holy Week, and
never have I experienced the truth of the Resurrection
so profoundly.

It is all here in our days on earth: sorrow and joy,
life and death, all mixed together, one following upon
the other.

There is such a mystery to it all, one that we see
embodied in the life, death, and resurrection of Jesus.
Our savior, Lord, and brother—born and put to death.
And risen.

*Loving God, in hopeful faith I offer to you all my
sorrows and joys.*

April 12

Jesus said, "Leave her alone. She bought it
so that she might keep it for the day of
my burial. You always have the poor with
you, but you do not always have me."

—JOHN 12:7–8

Mary, the sister of Martha and Lazarus, anoints
Jesus and is scolded by Judas for the waste.

This act, as John makes clear in his Gospel, is
profoundly spiritual. Mary is symbolically anointing
Jesus for his burial, revealing her own insight into
Jesus' identity and mission.

Sometimes, in the midst of a busy day, taking a
moment or even longer to be consciously in the presence of the Lord seems like a waste of time. Surely I
could be doing other things. Surely there are other,
more important things to be done.

*Lord, help me listen to your promptings and take
time for you when you call.*

April 13

For I received from the Lord what I also handed on
to you, that the Lord Jesus on the night when he
was betrayed took a loaf of bread, and when he had
given thanks, he broke it and said, "This is my body
that is for you. Do this in remembrance of me."

—1 Corinthians 11:23–24

Have you ever drifted through your kitchen, just grazing? Have you ever wandered the grocery store, vaguely hungry but unable to commit? There's an emptiness inside—you know that—but what will satisfy it is another issue entirely.

Sometimes we drift in that same way through days, weeks, and months of life. We try this and that; we put our minds and hearts to various activities that we think will satisfy us. But we're still hungry. What can we find now that will fill us, at least for a while?

When we gather at the Lord's table, we come bearing our own hungers, some we can articulate and others we cannot. We are grieving, lost, confused, and lonely. But we all have ended up at the same place, looking to the same bread to feed us.

The miracle is that God will feed and satisfy us.

*Lord, thank you for the gift of yourself in
the Eucharist.*

April 14

Let the same mind be in you that was in
Christ Jesus,
who, though he was in the form of God,
did not regard equality with God
as something to be exploited,
but emptied himself,
taking the form of a slave,
being born in human likeness.
And being found in human form,
he humbled himself
and became obedient to the point of death—
even death on a cross.

—PHILIPPIANS 2:5–8

Someone once pointed out to me how much time
we spend in front of televisions and computer
screens trying to be smarter, trying to figure out
how to live. Instead, we could spend fifteen minutes
meditating on the crucified Jesus.

Which would bear more fruit?

Jesus, open my spirit to the mystery of your cross.

April 15

When the sabbath was over, Mary Magdalene, and
Mary the mother of James, and Salome bought
spices, so that they might go and anoint him.

—MARK 16:1

They have been there for a long time—the women
who followed Jesus from Nazareth to Jerusalem,
who remained faithful at the cross, and finally, who
ventured to the tomb.

Again and again we've heard this story. Those the
world puts last, those of whom it expects least, those it
even confines—those are the ones whom God chooses
to witness most profoundly to his love and mercy.

And the world watches, astonished, wondering
what else it has missed along the way.

Lord, give me the courage to be faithful.

If Christ has not been raised, then our proclamation
has been in vain and your faith has been in vain.

—1 CORINTHIANS 15:14

I'll admit that I still am seized, once in a while, with
a fear of death. Some days I'm okay, but there are
others on which the obituary page or a traffic stop
alongside a cemetery fills me with dread.

I don't want to go.

But those are the days I must really listen with
my whole being to Paul and revisit, sometimes step-
by-step, everything I know to be true. Yes, Jesus rose.
Yes, these witnesses were telling the truth. Yes, this is
about me, as well, and about all of creation, mysteriously, now and forever.

Alleluia!

*Lord Jesus, may the hope of eternity in your presence
govern my life today and always.*

Jesus said to her, "Woman, why are you weeping?
Whom are you looking for?" Supposing him to
be the gardener, she said to him, "Sir, if you have
carried him away, tell me where you have laid
him, and I will take him away." Jesus said to her,
"Mary!" She turned and said to him in Hebrew,
"Rabbouni!" (which means Teacher).

—JOHN 20:15–16

One night, when my son was about a year old, I
had a rare reprieve from duty to take a shower.
I returned downstairs a few minutes later to find my
son happily playing with my husband. The baby looked
up at me. His eyes slowly widened, his smile collapsed,
he turned to his father, and he started wailing. Why?
My hair was wrapped up in a towel on top of my head.
He didn't recognize me. Until I spoke his name.

Every Gospel account of the risen Jesus tells us
that he was the same Jesus but appeared different
somehow. So different that even Mary Magdalene,
who knew him well, couldn't recognize him—until he
spoke her name.

*Jesus, in the quiet of my heart, I hear you speak my
name, and I know you.*

April 18

"Therefore let the entire house of Israel know with
certainty that God has made him both Lord and
Messiah, this Jesus whom you crucified."
Now when they heard this, they were cut to the
heart and said to Peter and to the other apostles,
"Brothers, what should we do?"

—ACTS 2:36–37

The good news is preached to me, as well. Jesus is
Lord and Christ. He will save me. I need no one
and nothing else to rescue me from my own darkness,
pain, and fear.

I've heard. Now, what must I do?

*Lord, today I lay a painful part of my life at your
feet. Save me.*

April 19

When he was at the table with them, he took bread,
blessed and broke it, and gave it to them. Then
their eyes were opened, and they recognized him;
and he vanished from their sight.

—LUKE 24:30–31

Mass can be a distracting time, Sunday Mass in
particular—with the crowds, the announce-
ments, the various groups making appeals for money
or members, not to speak of the distractions of my
own family.

With so much going on, it can be easy to forget
that this is all about Jesus. But he waits, quietly, amid
the ruckus, in the mystery of bread and wine that are
his body and blood given for all his distractible, distracting children.

*Jesus, open my heart to the gift of yourself
in Eucharist.*

April 20

Now there was an Ethiopian eunuch, a court
official of the Candace, queen of the Ethiopians,
in charge of her entire treasury. He had come
to Jerusalem to worship and was returning home;
seated in his chariot, he was reading the prophet
Isaiah. Then the Spirit said to Philip, "Go over
to this chariot and join it."

—ACTS 8:27–29

At first glance, it seems odd—that on the road from
Jerusalem, Philip would meet the official in
charge of the Ethiopian court treasury reading the
Hebrew Scriptures.

There are times when I get far too settled in my
own ways of seeing things. I'm so absorbed in figuring
out God's ways in my own life and habits that I look
at others and see nothing or no one worth noting.
Yet what I should see are my brothers and sisters on
the same journey as I, with the same God moving in
their hearts.

What am I missing when I close myself off from
the unexpected? Who else is journeying down the road?

*Jesus, send your Spirit, and lead me to where I'm
needed today.*

April 21

For this reason I bow my knees before the Father, from whom every family in heaven and on earth takes its name. I pray that, according to the riches of his glory, he may grant that you may be strengthened in your inner being with power through his Spirit, and that Christ may dwell in your hearts through faith, as you are being rooted and grounded in love.

—EPHESIANS 3:14–17

Perhaps there has been a moment when your heart practically burst with love. You see your spouse or best friend after a long absence, or even first thing in the morning. You hold a new baby or say good-bye to your grown-up child.

At that moment, nothing else seems possible or real, except love.

That is what Paul is talking about; that is his prayer for the Ephesians, and for you and me. That God might fill us, so that life is filled with the possibility and hope of the love that is perfect and never ends. So that there is room for nothing else.

God, fill me.

April 22

Although you have not seen him, you love him;
and even though you do not see him now, you
believe in him and rejoice with an indescribable
and glorious joy, for you are receiving the outcome
of your faith, the salvation of your souls.

—1 PETER 1:8–9

Our relationship with God is like all things human.
It can wither on the vine.

Which is one of the reasons, I suppose, that we
follow the journeys of those seeking to be joined to
Christ so closely and publicly in our church. Through
the catechumenate, and then through the beautiful
moments at the Easter Vigil and beyond, we're blessed
to be in the presence of those who are deeply conscious
of that joy of which Peter speaks.

I know that all it takes to revive my flagging faith
is one glance at the happy face of a person who's been
newly reborn in Christ. He or she reminds me: *It's
real. He changes your life.*

*Lord, I pray for all who are journeying to you, and I
thank you for their witness.*

April 23

Now the eleven disciples went to Galilee,
to the mountain to which Jesus had
directed them. When they saw him, they
worshiped him; but some doubted.

—MATTHEW 28:16–17

I find this one of the most fascinating passages in the Gospels. It's one of those small, absolutely honest moments one finds throughout Scripture, moments that attest, at least in my mind, to the essential authenticity of the witness. You don't add this sort of detail to something you've fabricated:

". . . some doubted."

Matthew doesn't specify what they doubt. The identity of this man as Jesus? The meaning of his presence?

Most of us have moments of doubt, and hiding them doesn't help. God wants us to belong to him completely. Every bit. Even our doubts.

Lord, I believe. Help my unbelief.

April 24

There was not a needy person among them,
for as many as owned lands or houses sold them
and brought the proceeds of what was sold.

—ACTS 4:34

As a Christian in America, I'm surrounded by competing philosophies. Faced with want, what do I say? Shall I watch from a distance and applaud as people pull themselves up by their bootstraps?

Or do I ponder what these Jerusalem Christians did and say—and perhaps even do—something else?

Lord, open my eyes to the want around me, and empower me to help.

April 25

But they covered their ears, and with a loud
shout all rushed together against him.

—ACTS 7:57

It is St. Stephen under attack here, and sadly enough, it is religious leaders who have "covered their ears," unwilling to listen to truth.

There's no doubt that facing the truth can be painful. There are times when the phone rings, and I dread picking it up because I just know it's one of my young-adult sons, deep in a mess I can't fix. Or I see the look on my daughter's face when she comes home from school, and I think, *I can't. I can't hear about what mean girls have done to you today. It hurts too much and makes me too angry. Can't we just pretend?*

No, we can't. And if we're honest, we'll admit that we don't want to pretend, anyway. We know that the only real, lasting joy comes from living in the truth. Even if we have to walk through pain first.

*Lord, give me the courage to face a painful
truth today.*

April 26

The women were terrified and bowed their faces
to the ground, but the men said to them, "Why
do you look for the living among the dead? He
is not here, but has risen."

—LUKE 24:5

How much of my life is spent trying to make up
for the past or remake the past in some way?
Why do I do this?

With Christ living within me in the present, there's
no reason to keep dredging up the past. It's dead.

*Jesus, fill me with your Spirit and give me hope in
the present.*

Yet more than ever believers were added to the
Lord, great numbers of both men and women,
so that they even carried out the sick into the
streets, and laid them on cots and mats, in
order that Peter's shadow might fall on some
of them as he came by.

—ACTS 5:14–15

I was once at a small-group gathering at which a
woman was lamenting the dryness of her spiritual
life. "I've been involved in church for ages," she said.
"I've been on the liturgy committee and the parish
council and everything else, it seems. But I still feel
empty. I wish I could feel closer to God."

When I ponder the early Christian community as
described in Acts, somehow committee work doesn't
jump out at me as an identifying point. It's surely not
why others were drawn to this community.

Discipleship doesn't close us up on ourselves. It
draws us out, to witness to the world.

Lord, lead me out into the world to share your love.

April 28

While they were talking about this,
Jesus himself stood among them and
said to them, "Peace be with you."

—LUKE 24:36

When will this peace that Jesus promises arrive?
When I get all my tasks completed? When I'm certain that I'm spiritually complete and morally beyond reproach? What do I have to do to know Christ's peace?

Nothing. I don't have to do anything. I can't. And that's the point. In the midst of it all, Jesus' peace awaits—the peace that's rooted in completely trusting God.

Lord, open my heart to your peace.

April 29

St. Catherine of Siena

The wicked flee when no one pursues,
but the righteous are as bold as a lion.
—Proverbs 28:1

St. Catherine of Siena is my daughter's patron saint, along with St. Louise de Marillac, and one day when she was about seven, I was reading to her about the life of St. Catherine.

This particular story focused on St. Catherine's austerities: how she slept on a board for only an hour a night, how little she ate, and so on. My daughter, who was deciding which saint to dress up as for her school's All Saints' Day pageant, took all this tough, strange stuff into consideration.

Finally, she decided. "I wanna be St. Louise."

There's more to St. Catherine than asceticism, of course. There's wisdom and courage and single-minded love for God. All in the package of an uneducated, medieval laywoman.

Wonderful. But daunting, too.

Lord, dispel my fear as I shape my life in imitation of your holy ones.

April 30

See what love the Father has given us,
that we should be called children of God;
and that is what we are.

—1 JOHN 3:1

Our zoo opens in late spring. We have a membership and an energetic toddler, so Joseph and I go to the zoo at least once a week.

What I love most (besides the wearing-out-the-toddler factor) is to see the animal mothers and their babies: the ducklings and goslings following their mothers in straight, little lines; the capuchin monkey babies clinging to their mothers' backs; the joeys, their long feet sticking out from kangaroo pouches.

It is a little world of absolute trust born of instinct, the gift of God to his beloved creatures so that they might grow and flourish.

Heavenly Father, I trust in your care and love for me.

May

May 1

Then God said, "Let us make humankind in our
image, according to our likeness; and let them
have dominion over the fish of the sea, and over
the birds of the air, and over the cattle, and over
all the wild animals of the earth, and over every
creeping thing that creeps upon the earth."

—GENESIS 1:26

In a world that seems to value leisure above all else,
how countercultural of us to celebrate work!

But we might consider that work is part of our
makeup, that it's actually part of the divine image
within us. As a writer, sitting before a blinking,
expectant computer screen, I would prefer that it not
be the case. But—too bad.

When we work out of commitment, imagination,
and service, we are, in a way, like God. God created.
We create. God's creation is a gift to those he loves,
as is ours. God's creation is an expression of his love,
care, and responsibility. Upon completion, I, too, can
rest, pleased with what my hands have wrought, and
declare, like God, that "it is good!"

*Lord, thank you for the gift of work. May my work
bring me closer to you.*

May 2

A certain woman named Lydia, a worshiper
of God, was listening to us; she was from the
city of Thyatira and a dealer in purple cloth.
The Lord opened her heart to listen eagerly to
what was said by Paul.

—Acts 16:14

None of my babies have been good sleepers. When they're little, I see a lot of the middle of the night. What always fascinates me is the quiet. It's so still that when a train passes on tracks two miles away, it sounds as if it's in our backyard. I suppose this shows me that there's a lot more noise out there during the day than I realize.

When we pray, we may be convinced that we're listening to God. But are we? Or have we just grown so accustomed to the continual drone that we don't even know it's there, muffling and distorting God's voice? And then we're startled when God's voice resounds like a train through the night, unfamiliar but at last unmistakable, and we must, like Lydia, open our hearts and listen eagerly.

Loving God, help me really quiet myself and listen.

May 3

"The God who made the world and everything
in it, he who is Lord of heaven and earth, does
not live in shrines made by human hands."

—ACTS 17:24

One day in Athens, Paul preached about idols. A thing of the past? Maybe.

Is there something in life of which you ask: "Give me peace. Don't fail me. Sustain me in the darkness. Assure me that I'm valued. Love me always. Make my life meaningful"?

If that something or someone isn't God, it's an idol. If I insist, beyond all rationality, that the things and people of this world bear infinite weight, then I honor idols.

We are also like the Athenians, as Paul notes, in knowing that there is indeed more: an unknown God who sustains it all. Can I cast aside the idols and worship the true God at last?

*Lord, help me see that my yearnings are really
yearnings for you.*

May 4

Jesus said to them, "I am the bread of life.
Whoever comes to me will never be hungry, and
whoever believes in me will never be thirsty."

—JOHN 6:35

❖

The Scriptures are filled with meal imagery, but a parent, especially one who cooks, may have to work through some issues when she's presented with the possibility that heaven is like a never-ending meal. An eternity of children picking unenthusiastically at food you've spent hours preparing? A forever filled with sibling squabbles and spilled milk?

Do I really have to go?

Oh, but then we retrieve other memories. The countless, uneventful meals that built a family. Moments when, out of the blue, restless children were transformed into young women and men, lingering over the meal, actually conversing, and enjoying it. The times someone said "thank you"—and meant it.

Heaven is a feast, and Jesus is the bread of life. The good moments give me a glimpse of what that means.

Yes, I want to go.

Jesus, fill me with the bread that satisfies and binds me to you and your children.

May 5

For three days he was without sight,
and neither ate nor drank.

—ACTS 9:9

Saul never could have imagined what was coming. When the transformation began, the impact was almost too much. Mystery enfolded him as he waited in darkness—for what, he didn't know.

The past, however, was not wasted. His rabbinical training had made him conversant in the law. His youth in the busy port of Tarsus exposed him to many cultures. And both, combined with Paul's God-given brilliance and strength, worked within God's plan to bring the Gospel to the entire world, Jew and gentile alike.

It works this way for each of us. The road ahead is filled with surprises, but we walk in confidence, knowing that even if we're in the dark, all that has happened before can be used for our growth and God's glory.

Lord, help me see every moment of my life as a step closer to you.

May 6

> "I have come as light into the world,
> so that everyone who believes in me
> should not remain in the darkness."

—JOHN 12:46

My daughter hesitates at the foot of the stairs. She didn't argue when we suggested she go do her homework. But now, confronted with the only way to get there, she pauses, peering up at the dark at the top of the stairs. She doesn't say anything, because she doesn't care to hear another word about groundless fears for a nine-year-old. And the thing is, she really does know that there's nothing to fear. But she doesn't believe it.

I know the light that Jesus gives me will over-power the darkness. But do I pause at the brink, afraid to believe it?

Jesus, deepen my faith in the power of your light.

He went into all the region around the Jordan,
proclaiming a baptism of repentance for the
forgiveness of sins.

—LUKE 3:3

A priest once told me that, in his experience, people
have felt more guilt for violating their diets than
they have for committing sins.

Hmm.

*Forgiving God, I admit my wrongdoing before you,
hopeful for your mercy.*

May 8

So they left the tomb quickly with fear and
great joy, and ran to tell his disciples.

—MATTHEW 28:8

One year, we attended Easter Vigil at a Benedictine monastery, which is a lot more complicated than it sounds. For, you see, they do it in two parts. They start at night with the Liturgy of the Word, retire for rest and private prayer, then come back at 5 AM—yes!—for the rest of Mass.

Even through my blurry-eyed fatigue, I was struck by two components of the liturgy. First was the presentation of a real, live lamb, in a basket, to the abbot. The second occurred when the assisting minister entered and announced to the abbot that he had good news—"The tomb is empty, and Jesus is risen!"

As if it had just happened, for us, here and now.

Jesus, you live among us here and now. Open our hearts to that presence and its possibilities.

May 9

He heals the brokenhearted,
and binds up their wounds.

—PSALM 147:3

It was one of those terrible nights, one of those it-all-comes-down-to-this arguments with my oldest son. The reason for all his problems, his attitude, and his struggles: Me. Me and my decisions.

I wasn't unprepared, and I didn't argue with his perspective. But I did say this:

You're not alone. Everyone looks at every other family and sees perfect happiness. It's just not so. Every single family, every single person has something deep inside that hurts, that tempts us to think: *If only this situation had been different, I'd be happier. I'd be more able to get it together.*

It's what binds us: how we've been let down, and how we've let others down. No one is immune. But neither is any of this hurt too much for God to heal.

Lord, take up my hurt in your loving embrace.

May 10

Whoever is slow to anger has great understanding,
but one who has a hasty temper exalts folly.
—PROVERBS 14:29

I am not the most patient person in the world, and whenever I am tempted to lose it, I think of the Amish woman at the airport.

She was going through security and she set off the alarm. Repeatedly. They ran the wand over her, back and forth, although she assured them she had no metal on her. And still she beeped.

Watching this, I was relieved that so much energy was being exerted to protect me from the dangers of fifty-year-old Amish women. But I also had to admire her patience: there was no logical reason to keep examining and searching her, and it was even a little insulting. But through it all, her smile never faded, for, as she probably well understood, anger would have accomplished nothing.

Loving God, build up my patience.

May 11

When it was evening on that day, the first day
of the week, and the doors of the house where
the disciples had met were locked for fear of
the Jews, Jesus came and stood among them
and said, "Peace be with you."

—JOHN 20:19

If there's one thing that saddens me, it's a church
with locked doors.

Oh, I understand the reasons—safety, security,
and so on—but still, it doesn't seem right. It seems
that if we are who we say we are, and if we belong to
Christ, our doors should always be open.

Not to speak of our hearts and lives, too.

*Jesus, fill me with your peace, so that I might open
the door of my heart to you and to others.*

May 12

When the Spirit of truth comes, he will guide you
into all the truth; for he will not speak on his
own, but will speak whatever he hears, and he will
declare to you the things that are to come.
—John 16:13

When my daughter was a toddler, we were living in Florida, where small lizards are as common as ants. We were on the back porch getting some sun, when a lizard scampered up near us and froze, its throat heaving.

My daughter looked at it. "Dinosaur," she decided.

"No," I answered. "It's a lizard."

"Dinosaur," she insisted. I let it rest. At the time I was dealing with my own set of problems, which seemed rather monstrous. I had to wonder if those problems really were dinosaurs or just lizards, not nearly the threat that I imagined them to be.

Jesus, fill me with your spirit, so that I might discern the true nature of the problems in my life.

May 13

By faith Abraham obeyed when he was called
to set out for a place that he was to receive as
an inheritance; and he set out, not knowing
where he was going.

—HEBREWS 11:8

One cool Saturday in November, we were in a rented car, driving around Manhattan. We wanted to get to the other side of Central Park, but my husband didn't want to go around. "I'm pretty sure you can drive through it," he declared, and then he found his opening, a road on the south end.

In vain, I pointed out a barrier that had been pushed a bit to the side but was definitely intended to block traffic. "I don't think you're supposed to—" but it was too late. We quickly figured out the error, being the only car on paths crowded with runners, walkers, bikers, and skaters. That we didn't get a ticket was some sort of miracle.

We may not always know where we're going. But God never fails to give us signs along the way. We have to pay attention, though, to see them.

Father, help me be guided by the signs you will give me today.

May 14

When they had finished breakfast, Jesus said to
Simon Peter, "Simon son of John, do you love me
more than these?" He said to him, "Yes, Lord;
you know that I love you." Jesus said to him,
"Feed my lambs." A second time he said to him,
"Simon son of John, do you love me?" He said
to him, "Yes, Lord; you know that I love you."
Jesus said to him, "Tend my sheep."

—JOHN 21:15–16

We could spend our lives reading books, listening
to tapes, attending lectures, and hoping to
understand what it means to follow Jesus. What does
a disciple look like? How does a disciple live?

The better question is why do we insist on making the answer so complicated?

Lord, I love you. Live in me today as I share your love.

May 15

Then he said, "Jesus, remember me when you come into your kingdom." He replied, "Truly I tell you, today you will be with me in Paradise."

—LUKE 23:42–43

Flipping through the radio stations, my husband chanced upon a religious discussion. The host, guest, and callers were arguing about the fate of the good thief crucified with Jesus, each side providing all kinds of arcane arguments over the precise mechanics of how the thief could have been saved. Jesus' promise to the thief seemed to weigh little in the discussion.

My husband and I thought the same thing at the same time: "This is why people get turned off by religion." The temptation to use our God-given minds to dice up religious matters into tiny points is irresistible, but it can often work not to enlighten but to distract us from what God wants us to take to heart.

God of wisdom, for a moment, I set aside my questions and just listen.

May 16

"I do not call you servants any longer, because
the servant does not know what the master is
doing; but I have called you friends, because I
have made known to you everything that I
have heard from my Father."

—JOHN 15:15

There is a part of me, deep down, that stubbornly doesn't want to believe that God is on my side. I don't know where it comes from, but it's the suspicion that God is always watching and waiting for me to mess up or fall, not because he wants to punish me but more for a good laugh and to expose me for what I really am.

Jesus affirms our friendship here; in fact, he defines his relationship with us primarily as a friendship. Which is not distance and bemusement, but love, compassion—and support.

Jesus, deepen my awareness of your faithful
friendship in my life.

May 17

Then he appeared to more than five hundred
brothers and sisters at one time, most of
whom are still alive, though some have died.

—1 CORINTHIANS 15:6

When I was about thirteen years old, my pre-viously clean-shaven father grew a handlebar mustache and took to wearing striped, bell-bottom pants (it was 1973).

I was distressed, and actually a little bit angry. I remember thinking—although I don't know if I ever said it out loud—that he just didn't look like a Dad anymore.

The Gospels and Paul tell us that after the Resurrection, Jesus appeared to many. All who saw him had some difficulty recognizing or accepting him. Their faith had to take them a step or two beyond their previous experience and expectations in order to really see Jesus.

When I look, is there something preventing me from seeing Jesus for who he is?

Lord Jesus, bring me closer to you in faith.

May 18

But they kept asking him, "Then how were your
eyes opened?" He answered, "The man called
Jesus made mud, spread it on my eyes, and said
to me, 'Go to Siloam and wash.' Then I went
and washed and received my sight." They said to
him, "Where is he?" He said, "I do not know."

—JOHN 9:10–12

This conversation is the first of several the man
has after Jesus has healed him. He's beset from all
sides by questioners who want to know who did this
and how. Here, the man admits he knows nothing,
only that he's been healed. What fascinates me is
that, as each set of questioners challenges him, his
understanding grows. By the end, when Jesus himself
seeks this man out again, he affirms Jesus as Lord.

This incident shows me how important it is to
open myself to questions and conversations about
faith, and not to isolate myself in a self-referential cave,
conversing only with those I'm sure will agree with
me. In fact, I don't remember ever growing much—or
seeing more clearly—as a result of that.

*Lord Jesus, heal me of my blindness, and take me
into the world.*

May 19

They show that what the law requires is
written on their hearts, to which their
own conscience also bears witness.

—ROMANS 2:15

I have a theory. I really think that at every step of
the way and with every choice we make, God has
something to say about it.

In fact, when I look back at my life, at some
major sins and bad choices I've been guilty of, I can
say pretty confidently that I intuited or just plain
knew what the right choice was. But I ignored it. I
may try, but I can never honestly claim ignorance.
Just weakness and a stubborn heart.

*Lord, in the quiet, I examine my conscience and let
you strengthen me to make life-giving choices.*

May 20

"Very truly, I tell you, unless a grain of wheat falls
into the earth and dies, it remains just a single
grain; but if it dies, it bears much fruit."

—John 12:24

In the world's eyes, death is the end. In the kingdom
where God reigns, death is an opportunity for
God's power to bring forth life.

And that goes for every death I may experience
today—every end of every single road, every disappointment. What do I do with those deaths? Do I
let them bury me, or do I hand them over to God and
say, "Here—I trust that there is life. Even here"?

*Lord, help me see the possibilities of life in every
small death I experience.*

May 21

O come, let us worship and bow down,
let us kneel before the LORD, our Maker!
—PSALM 95:6

I once took a group of high-school students to a retreat day at a nearby monastery. Part of the day involved attendance at Mass.

Afterward, some students remarked that the experience had been different from Mass at their home parishes. "Here, it was like the focus was all on God. At home, it's more like it's all about us."

What's my focus when I go to Mass? Is it about me, or is it actually about God?

Lord, I praise and thank you.

May 22

His disciples did not understand these things
at first; but when Jesus was glorified, then they
remembered that these things had been written
of him and had been done to him.

—JOHN 12:16

When my youngest son was first starting to speak, we could understand almost everything he said, except one word: "Ernst." He would go into the kitchen, stand and point, "Ernst!" He'd pound on the refrigerator, "Ernst!" He'd jump in front of the pantry, "Ernst!" We were totally baffled. I would go through lists of food, and nothing was right. "Ernst!"

Until finally, one day, he put it in context for us. He toddled into the kitchen, as usual, and said, "Somepin' ernst!" Ah—something *else*. I repeated it to him, and he nodded, obviously relieved that someone finally got it.

Sometimes, when we listen to Jesus' words, they are almost impossible to understand. But then, when the totality of his life, death, and resurrection put it in context for us, we can finally get it.

Jesus, immerse me in the fullness of your life so that I might understand.

May 23

The Lord said:
Because these people draw near with their mouths
and honor me with their lips,
while their hearts are far from me,
and their worship of me is a human commandment
learned by rote;
so I will again do
amazing things with this people,
shocking and amazing.

—ISAIAH 29:13–14

Religion has been my business, in some form or another, my entire adult life.

And as anyone who works in a church or religious organization can tell you, there's hardly anything more dangerous to one's faith than that.

They'll tell you how over time the initial fire and excitement can drain away. It can become just one more job, learned by rote, hollowed out by routine.

You don't have to work in a church to experience it, I suppose. Any of us can get into a rut, distancing what we say we believe from the way we live.

Lord, amaze me again with the power of your love.

May 24

Finally, beloved, whatever is true, whatever is
honorable, whatever is just, whatever is pure,
whatever is pleasing, whatever is commendable,
if there is any excellence and if there is anything
worthy of praise, think about these things.

—PHILIPPIANS 4:8

I don't think Paul is asking us to mindlessly accentu-
ate the positive or deny reality. Paul, more than most
people, understood suffering, pain, and difficulty.

But in faith, we believe that in any circumstance
God is present, somewhere and somehow.

Paul is saying that God's presence is just as much
a part of the situation as anything else. Where's our
focus? What do we see?

*Loving God, help me see your handprint in my
life today.*

May 25

While he was going and they were gazing up
toward heaven, suddenly two men in white
robes stood by them. They said, "Men of Galilee,
why do you stand looking up toward heaven?
This Jesus, who has been taken up from you into
heaven, will come in the same way as you saw
him go into heaven."

—ACTS 1:10–11

Spiritual nostalgia can be hard to resist. For the
last two decades of her life, my mother lived in
constant yearning for the old Latin Mass. I sometimes
look back in fondness at the close community of
my college years or the times I've spent in monastic
environments.

That's real spirituality, we think. God was really
there, no doubt about that.

The point of Jesus' ascension is, of course, the
exact opposite. No longer bound by limitations of
time and space, he is with us always.

*Lord, help me see the fullness of your loving presence
in the here and now.*

May 26

Meanwhile the church throughout Judea, Galilee, and Samaria had peace and was built up. Living in the fear of the Lord and in the comfort of the Holy Spirit, it increased in numbers.

—ACTS 9:31

Out in a public place, sometimes we hear a baby or toddler start to cry. My son Joseph, who is no baby anymore, gets a funny look on his face, listens, and then utters this faint, very fake-sounding cry, half-grimacing, half-smiling.

And he's not the only one. Crying babies beget more crying babies in a chain reaction of imitation and sympathy.

So it is with a people alive in Christ. Who can turn away from such a people, committed and vibrant with God's love, without feeling the pull to share in the joy?

Jesus, fill me with your spirit so my life might draw others to you.

May 27

I do not cease to give thanks for you
as I remember you in my prayers.
—EPHESIANS 1:16

I can't even name all the people who have helped me grow in my faith—living and dead, people I knew well, and some I never met.

But I'm grateful for their presence and for all the ways that God worked through them, whether I understood it at the time or not.

Father, thank you for all who have helped me grow in faith.

May 28

Then Jesus asked, "Were not ten made clean? But the other nine, where are they? Was none of them found to return and give praise to God except this foreigner?" Then he said to him, "Get up and go on your way; your faith has made you well."
—LUKE 17:17–19

They call it *morning sickness*, but that's a dirty lie. For me at least, during those first months of pregnancy (which I happen to be in right now, again), it's all day, every day, stomach-churning queasiness.

I know it's for a good cause—the best cause of all, as a matter of a fact. But that doesn't prevent me from yearning for a day of a settled stomach and promising I'll never take such a blissful physical state for granted, ever again.

Sure. That will happen.

Lord God, in the quiet, I count my blessings and thank you for them.

May 29

Three times I appealed to the Lord about this,
that it would leave me, but he said to me,
"My grace is sufficient for you, for power is
made perfect in weakness." So, I will boast
all the more gladly of my weaknesses, so
that the power of Christ may dwell in me.

—2 Corinthians 12:8–9

In my view at least, my greatest spiritual weakness is a nagging doubt. It's rooted mostly in my questions and my inability (or unwillingness) to shut my intellect off and just . . . leap.

I'm rather bothered by that, but less so since the day when I realized that in this weakness is a cross for me, and that God wants me to use it as a blessing for others. For as I seek out the answers to my questions, I help others answer their questions. It also gives me insight into the minds of skeptics and the more serious, thorough doubters, which is really important for a person who does what I do—write about faith in a way that's not just preaching to the choir.

It's still frustrating, but if I can let God work through it—well, God will work.

Lord, use my weakness for your glory.

May 30

"So you also, when you have done all that you
were ordered to do, say, 'We are worthless slaves;
we have done only what we ought to have done!'"
—LUKE 17:10

❧

I sometimes try to calculate out how many school
lunches I've packed over twenty years of parenting.
Then, since my youngest is two, and I'm expecting
another, I add another eighty years' worth to the total,
and come out of the exercise wondering what forty
years of lunches will be worth in the end.

And then I stop, before I get too depressed.

In today's reading, Jesus asks his disciples to consider whether a servant should expect gratitude for
doing what was expected. The hard answer is, no. But
for the disciple of Jesus, who sees God in all things,
the obligation is not drudgery. It is a gift—the gift of
sharing love because we have been loved first.

And love comes in all shapes and sizes, even in
brown-paper bags. Lots of them.

*Lord, thank you for the opportunity to serve you
through loving others.*

May 31

VISITATION

When Elizabeth heard Mary's greeting, the child
leaped in her womb. And Elizabeth was filled with
the Holy Spirit and exclaimed with a loud cry,
"Blessed are you among women, and blessed is
the fruit of your womb."

—LUKE 1:41–42

The Gospels aren't only about Jesus. They are just
as much about how people respond to Jesus and,
implicitly, to God's presence in their lives.

It startles me to look at the whole range of responses to Jesus in the Gospels and to note that the last
person to respond to Jesus in faith during his earthly
lifetime was a criminal being publicly executed. And,
as we are reminded on this Feast of the Visitation, the
first to respond to him was an unborn child.

Jesus, I love you.

June

June 1

How could we sing the LORD's song
in a foreign land?

—PSALM 137:4

The psalmist sings of exile, that of the people of Israel to Babylon in the sixth century BC. The lament is born of grief, rage, and loss.

Our exiles are different, but they are just as real. We grow into a relationship with God assuming certain things: I know God loves me because he's blessed me with health, with family, with talent.

But what happens when illness strikes? Divorce and death? When our talents are unappreciated and ignored? In those situations, we're ripped from the ground in which our faith has grown, and we wonder how we can recover and sing the Lord's songs again.

Lord, help me to use the uncertainties in my life to nurture faith.

June 2

We ponder your steadfast love, O God,
in the midst of your temple.

—PSALM 48:9

Some Sunday mornings, I seem to do everything during Mass but ponder the kindness of God, distracted continually by what I've decided are the needs of those around me.

I look at my sons meaningfully, sending them telepathic threats about their posture and their participation. I soothe my daughter's hurt feelings after I whisper that no, she can't hold the baby right now, for I can see that the baby is toddling on the edge of hysteria and will plunge right over if he's removed from my lap.

Surrounded by distractions, I can't pray. But whose fault is that?

Could it be mine, since I've chosen, for that hour, to define those who are so close to the center of my life as distractions?

Lord, help me focus on your presence as I worship and as I live and work in the world.

June 3

Remember Jesus Christ, raised from the dead,
a descendant of David—that is my gospel,
for which I suffer hardship, even to the point
of being chained like a criminal. But the word
of God is not chained.

—2 Timothy 2:8–9

Like any new teacher, I was initially awed by my responsibility. So much to teach, so little time! And I worried about the example I was setting. I was a religion teacher, and if I was short-tempered, even for a second, wouldn't my students lose their faith forever? Quite a heavy load for a twenty-five-year-old, bearing the salvation of all those souls.

In time, though, I learned. I had to balance the truth that my witness is important with the knowledge that God is still God—so I don't have to be. He isn't limited by anything—either by chains of metal or by the limitations of being human.

Lord help me trust that you are not limited by my limitations.

June 4

All scripture is inspired by God and is useful
for teaching, for reproof, for correction, and
for training in righteousness, so that everyone
who belongs to God may be proficient, equipped
for every good work.
—2 Timothy 3:16–17

My daughter attended an evangelical day care in which every lesson was filtered through the prism of the Bible. The words to traditional nursery rhymes and folk songs were replaced by Scripture verses, and the alphabet was taught by means of the first letter of a verse, which they would then memorize.

Too much? I don't know. Maybe it was a little too closed off from the wider world. But there was not a bad lesson there. All wisdom, no matter what the subject, is rooted in the truth that is God.

Father, I listen to your word, attentive.

June 5

I led them with cords of human kindness,
with bands of love.
I was to them like those
who lift infants to their cheeks.
I bent down to them and fed them.
—HOSEA 11:4

If I had just a little more control, I'd be happier. Sound familiar? How often we blame our misery on a lack of control over our lives. We need to get a handle on our schedules; we need to get more control over our family lives; we need to get healthier so we can have more control over our bodies and, ultimately, how and when we're going to die. If only we could control that.

But if I had all that control, would God love me any more? Or less?

Whether this day (or my life) is running like clockwork or is out of control, I remain God's beloved infant, raised to his cheeks and bathed by the warmth of his love and mercy.

Lord, embrace me today and always. I need it.

June 6

The LORD called me before I was born,
while I was in my mother's womb he named me.

—ISAIAH 49:1

When we consider holiness, sometimes we think it's all about meekness and quietude. Not so.

Contemplating saints, we see it all: the meek and the bold, the unfailingly polite and the direct to the point of rudeness, the retiring and the adventurous. We see the homemaker, the traveler, the politician, the teacher, the contemplative, the ruler, the artist, and the servant.

Our potential for holiness is unique. It's ours alone, a gift of God, and his call to us—before we were born.

Lord, free me from the world's expectations, so that I may grow into the person you want me to be.

June 7

Jesus said, "Let the little children come to me, and do not stop them; for it is to such as these that the kingdom of heaven belongs."
—MATTHEW 19:14

I have been blessed with generally happy children, and when they are really small, they are especially happy. Even sadness and frustration don't last long, and they go on their way, joyful and, most strikingly, open to whatever comes their way. Open, welcoming, and joyful. That's what I think of when I think of children.

My toddler, for example, was ecstatic all day yesterday because he got new socks. You'd think he'd won the lottery. He couldn't get over it—carried the pack around with him all day, counting them, explaining the colors to anyone who'd listen. New socks. That's all it took.

I always have to wonder, what happens to that simple joy?

Jesus, help me to recapture a joyful openness toward your presence in my life and in the world.

June 8

He was praying in a certain place, and after he had
finished, one of his disciples said to him, "Lord,
teach us to pray, as John taught his disciples."
He said to them, "When you pray, say:
Father, hallowed be your name.
Your kingdom come."

—LUKE 11:1–2

When I'm at a loss for how to pray, I put myself in
the company of the apostles, who asked Jesus
that very question. And then I listen to what he says.

Where does prayer start? Does it start with me
and my needs?

Doesn't seem to be the case, at least according to
Jesus. Prayer starts with an acknowledgment of God's
role in the universe and in my life.

Who's the center of my prayer? God or me?

Our Father . . .

June 9

So we are always confident; even though we know that while we are at home in the body we are away from the Lord—for we walk by faith, not by sight. Yes, we do have confidence, and we would rather be away from the body and at home with the Lord.

—2 Corinthians 5:6–8

A friend of mine once gave her opinion of the concept of reincarnation.

"I love life, but really, once is enough. I'll be ready to be with God and stay there!"

Heavenly Father, help me see my restlessness as a yearning to be home with you.

Search me, O God, and know my heart;
test me and know my thoughts.
See if there is any wicked way in me,
and lead me in the way everlasting.

—PSALM 139:23–24

A colleague of mine was handing back the first test of the year to a freshman religion class. They responded with outrage. She had marked answers wrong, as one generally does on tests.

"You can't do that!" they complained. "This is religion! There can't be any wrong answers!" What they meant was that the only "right answer" in religion should be their opinions, no matter what. There was no objective measure. No truth.

I wonder if I sometimes have that stance toward God. What I think and feel must be right, just because I'm thinking and feeling it. I'm reluctant to admit that God might know better.

Lord, teach me. Correct me.

June 11

The LORD is near to the brokenhearted,
and saves the crushed in spirit.
—PSALM 34:18

I was in the dentist's waiting room, listening to a jovial fellow talk to the receptionist about how great life was, how everything was going fantastically well. I thought, *That's nice and simple. Why does spirituality have to be so complicated sometimes? Why can't we just be happy and share that happiness?*

A moment later, a woman rushed in for her appointment. As it turned out, she was there on the wrong day. Her appointment was the following week. "Oh, I'm sorry," she said, "I just can't think straight. I was nine months pregnant, and last week the baby died inside me. They don't know why."

And she rushed back out.

I had the answer to my question.

Lord, I pray for all those living with the mystery of sorrow.

While they were eating, he took a loaf of bread,
and after blessing it he broke it, gave it to them,
and said, "Take; this is my body." Then he took
a cup, and after giving thanks he gave it to them,
and all of them drank from it. He said to them,
"This is my blood of the covenant, which is
poured out for many."

—MARK 14:22–24

We had attended Mass at another parish that
week and were discussing the experience on
our way to the car.

My daughter, just a few months past her first
communion, burst into the conversation. "That blood
of Christ was sweet and good!"

Indeed.

Jesus, thank you for the gift of yourself in Eucharist.

June 13

With all wisdom and insight he has made
known to us the mystery of his will.

—EPHESIANS 1:8–9

I was leading an inquiry session about the Catholic
faith, and a woman interested in the Catholic
Church was in attendance with her friend, an ex-
Catholic, now an evangelical Christian. The friend
wasn't hesitant to explain why she'd left Catholicism
a couple of decades before. It was, in her words, the
"superstition" that got her.

And then, near the end, this same woman asked
me, "How powerful is a Mass?" I didn't understand at
first but came to see that she wanted to know if having
a Mass said for her intentions would "work."

I asked her what her intention was, why she
wanted a Mass said for her.

"So I can find a husband," she said.

Our words don't speak nearly as loudly as
our needs.

*Lord, I put all my needs into your hands, trusting in
your will.*

June 14

Then Jesus said to his disciples, "Truly I tell
you, it will be hard for a rich person to enter
the kingdom of heaven."

—MATTHEW 19:23

Why does Jesus say this? What is the problem
with wealth?

It seems that the problem lies in what we believe
will save us. Materially comfortable and prosperous,
we easily forget how much we need God.

What do I think I must have or achieve today? If I
lost it all, from where would my satisfaction come?

Heavenly Father, teach me to be content in you.

June 15

"Come to me, all you that are weary and are carrying heavy burdens, and I will give you rest."
—MATTHEW 11:28

At the airport, a family from India was preparing to fly back home for a holiday. Unfortunately, their bags weighed too much, and they had to empty them of twenty pounds, right then and there, and do it quickly.

So they opened their massive bags and picked out clothes, which the skycap helpfully carried over to the scale at the ticket counter. It was all gauzy, silky material—saris and light trousers, none of them individually weighing much of anything. But taken together, their weight would have prevented a great journey.

Some of my burdens are heavy, some are light. But even the light ones I need to hand over to Jesus, for all together, I know how much they can weigh me down.

Jesus, take my burdens, large and small.

June 16

For this reason, since the day we heard it, we have not ceased praying for you and asking that you may be filled with the knowledge of God's will in all spiritual wisdom and understanding.

—Colossians 1:9

I have lots of nagging questions about prayer, and always have.

Then one day, a few years ago, my oldest son drove away, his car packed full, a grin on his face, college and life ahead of him. He turned the corner and was gone. That was it.

There was nothing left I could do to take care of him. But I still wanted to. I still had to, and there was no way I could because I wouldn't be there, and it wouldn't be right, besides. But, I realized, as the intellectual fog cleared and I saw the simple truth, God would take care of my son.

So I set aside my questions. And I learned to really pray.

Lord, I offer up my prayers, confident in your care.

June 17

> To do righteousness and justice is more
> acceptable to the LORD than sacrifice.
>
> —PROVERBS 21:3

❖

When she was about five, my daughter was caught in the act of scribbling on the bathroom mirror with lipstick, much to her dismay and her brother's delight (in catching her).

After being found out, Katie began to wail in her own defense, "But I did it for God!" What she had written on the mirror was "I love God." So that made it okay!

Using God as our defense when we've done something wrong. It's not unheard of, no matter how old you are.

❖

Heavenly Father, purify my motives and my actions.

June 18

I will delight in your statutes;
I will not forget your word.
—Psalm 119:16

When my youngest started crawling, I hauled out the playpen. No way. He'd have none of it.

A year later, desperate to be able to clean without the Wrecker coming right behind me, I pulled it out again. This time, at the ripe old age of two, Joseph sat himself down with the few toys I'd tossed in there, looked up at me, grinned, and played. For an hour. It was almost as if he welcomed the restriction of his choices. He could concentrate on what mattered.

I see God's guidance in the same way. No need for me to make the mistakes, proven time and again, to be mistakes. If I trust God, and trust that he's right, I can focus on the beauty that's before me, without fear.

God, give me the wisdom to see your guidance
as a gift.

June 19

"Why do you see the speck in your neighbor's eye,
but do not notice the log in your own eye?"

—LUKE 6:41

My daughter has met her match. Since the day she was born, the little girl has delighted in telling others what to do. With the birth of her younger brother, we all breathed a sigh of relief. Finally, she'd have someone to legitimately boss around.

Except that Joseph will not be bossed. He's stubborn and strong willed and believes that Katie should do what he wants, not the other way around. Which leads to strong complaints on her part: Joseph is always trying to tell her what to do. And, apparently, that's a bad thing now.

Could it be that the qualities I love criticizing the most are actually my own greatest weaknesses?

*Jesus, help me see myself and my own flaws
more honestly.*

But if you do not do this, you have sinned against the LORD; and be sure your sin will find you out.

—NUMBERS 32:23

The signs had been there for a few weeks, but I'd ignored them. Or had chosen to believe that things would take care of themselves and just go away.

But one evening, my son went into our utility room and alerted me, with a panicked shout, that things hadn't gone away. He was confronting a sharp-toothed, curious possum, the one responsible for tipping over our trash. I'd hoped it would just get bored with us, but instead, it had decided to come even closer.

Sin can be like that. I really hope it will go away, or that it might not affect me. But if I persist in ignoring it, I might be surprised one day to find how it's made itself at home.

Jesus, mold me as your disciple, in great ways and in small.

June 21

Then Peter came and said to him, "Lord, if another member of the church sins against me, how often should I forgive? As many as seven times?" Jesus said to him, "Not seven times, but, I tell you, seventy-seven times."

—MATTHEW 18:21–22

I've been hurt, and I've been wronged.
Is refusing to forgive really going to help?
What I have I got to lose?

Jesus, you forgave. Live in me so that I might forgive as well.

As you therefore have received Christ Jesus the
Lord, continue to live your lives in him.
—COLOSSIANS 2:6

The fellow who was cutting my son's hair was
being teased by his coworkers for an amusing
e-mail he'd sent around, one that contained a lot of
big words. They told him they never thought that he
knew words like that. "Hey!" he said, "I'm a good
speller! I may not act like it when I'm around y'all,
but I am!"

I had to wonder what a good speller acts like.

It got me thinking about my own presumed identity as a follower of Jesus. Are there times and places
when I'm comfortable walking openly as his disciple,
and other times that I'm not?

*Jesus, I love you. Give me the courage to act
like it, always.*

June 23

The point is this: the one who sows sparingly
will also reap sparingly, and the one who
sows bountifully will also reap bountifully.

—2 Corinthians 9:6

One day in May, when I was still teaching, I chatted with the woman who was providing lunch to the school that day, the proprietor of a local sandwich shop. I told her of my decision to leave teaching and make a go of it as a full-time freelance writer. Two minutes, conversation over.

About a month later, I was doing it—getting up each morning and pretending I was a real, live, full-time writer. Of course, I constantly sought distractions, and this day, I ended up in that same woman's shop for lunch. We talked briefly, and she pushed the sub over the counter to me. I took out my wallet, and she shook her head.

"No charge. Absolutely not. Take it for good luck—for a good start to your writing career."

I'm telling you, I'd probably spoken to her for a total of ten minutes in my entire life. And here she was, for some reason, making a little sacrifice to boost my confidence. It was generosity, vividly defined.

Lord, open my heart to give generously today.

June 24

BIRTH OF JOHN THE BAPTIST

All who heard them pondered them and said,
"What then will this child become?" For, indeed,
the hand of the Lord was with him.
—LUKE 1:66

Given a child in their old age, Elizabeth and Zechariah knew something was up. The child would be, let us say, unusual. A vigorous, brave prophet, wearing animal skins in the desert, dining on locusts, challenging the local king and losing his life for it.

If you're like me, faced with the unusual, you either avert your eyes or are morbidly fascinated. In either case, we're treating the unusual at a distance.

Not every unusual person is a prophet, but the sobering thing is, every prophet tends to be unusual.

Lord, help me see your presence in all things,
especially in people who make me feel uncomfortable.

You cause the grass to grow for the cattle,
and plants for people to use,
to bring forth food from the earth,
and wine to gladden the human heart,
oil to make the face shine,
and bread to strengthen the human heart.

—PSALM 104:14–15

I was running on the lake path near my house, with a million matters on my mind, a thousand tasks to complete before midnight. I really didn't think it showed.

A figure came around the bend. It was a very tall man, his body the definition of *pear shaped,* shuffling gamely along, bearing a broad, friendly grin. He drew nearer and then, before I knew it, shouted out a greeting.

"Life!" he called cheerfully as we passed. "Who knew it'd be so high maintenance?"

Who knew?

And who knew that God would offer himself as our very nourishment in this high-maintenance journey?

Jesus, I approach you in Eucharist, grateful as you feed my soul.

June 26

"He will reign over the house of Jacob forever,
and of his kingdom there will be no end."
—LUKE 1:33

When I go back to the city where I went to high school and college, I wonder where the time goes. But then I decide that it must go nowhere and everywhere at the same time.

I could walk into my old dorm room and feel as if I'd never left. I drive up to my parents' house, half expecting to see my mother as she was when we first looked at the place twenty-three years ago, with the chipmunk she had compassionately attempted to rescue from a lidless trash can hanging from the tip of her finger by its tiny, sharp teeth.

All of it still hovers, somehow, in something more than just my memory. When I walk those paths and experience the feeling of never having left, I think I understand, just a little, what eternity—the God's-eye view of life—might be.

Powerful, loving God, I ponder the mystery of life in you, now and forever.

June 27

I have indeed received much joy and
encouragement from your love.

—PHILEMON 7

I shouldn't have done it, but I did.

He'd left his religion-class journal on the table, so
I flipped it open and saw an entry written as a de-
scription of a time when he'd felt "desolation." It
revealed nothing I hadn't known, but before I shut
it, my eye fell on his final statement: "times when it
seemed like nobody else liked me, and my mom was
my only friend."

As it happens, the night before, we'd had one
of our huge, regularly scheduled arguments, during which he told me he hated me. I had fought the
feeling that I wasn't so wild about him either, even
though I hoped and prayed that every word I uttered
and everything I did communicated how much I
loved him.

Maybe, despite myself, it did.

*Jesus, love others through me, in my weakness
and my strength.*

June 28

From his fullness we have all received,
grace upon grace.

—JOHN 1:16

When I think of grace, this is how I think of it: as a gift that God is always, constantly offering to me.

But it's up to me to accept it. It's up to me not to just take the gift, store it on the top shelf of the closet, and forget about it.

But sometimes I do anyway. I wonder why.

Lord, help me discern what stops me from accepting the gift of your love in its fullness and in all its possibilities.

June 29

I, I am He
who blots out your transgressions for my own sake,
and I will not remember your sins.

—ISAIAH 43:25

In the part of the country where I live, winter lasts a long time, and everyone's ready to move to Florida by February. But then, by the second or third warm spring day, all is forgotten, and we think, *Well, this isn't so bad. In fact, it's pretty good!*

The same thing happens with childbirth. Unbearable at the time, forgotten almost as soon as it's over. So, I suspect, we will have more.

God says, just like that, he will forget my sins and let me start anew.

He can forget them, but can I?

Forgiving Lord, help me see myself as you see me. Forgiven.

"We played the flute for you, and you did not dance;
we wailed, and you did not mourn."
—MATTHEW 11:17

When my daughter was about three and I was a single, working mother having to get everyone up and out of the house by 7 AM, seemingly on principle, that little girl would find something to cry about.

Every morning. It was as if she'd signed a contract. She'd cry about her socks or her hair or the temperature or what she had for breakfast. Or something. She was committed, poor little thing, to find something to complain about, even if she had to make it happen herself.

Jesus wonders something similar about his listeners who, he notes, had complaints about John the Baptist's austerity and his own habit of eating with sinners. No matter what kind of person God sends, they grumble and find fault.

The whole time, not imagining what they have missed.

Jesus, help me find peace in the present and a reason for joy.

July

July 1

"But he replied, 'No; for in gathering the weeds
you would uproot the wheat along with them.
Let both of them grow together until the harvest;
and at harvest time I will tell the reapers, Collect
the weeds first and bind them in bundles to be
burned, but gather the wheat into my barn.'"

—MATTHEW 13:29–30

One of the most painful ways to spend your time, guaranteed, is to read over your adolescent diaries. I wasn't the most faithful journal keeper as a teen, but the record that remains is nothing but humiliating, and for one primary reason: I was a startlingly sanctimonious young lady, quick to judge others and bemoan my role as the only stalk of wheat in a field full of weeds.

Ah well, life has ways of dealing with that nasty, little flaw, and usually in short order. It's a painful lesson to learn: Our world is full of weeds and wheat, but we don't exactly have the breadth and depth of vision to separate them. Only God does.

Loving God, free me from the temptation to judge others, and strengthen me to leave the pruning of the weeds to you.

Then Amos answered Amaziah, "I am no
prophet, nor a prophet's son; but I am a
herdsman, and a dresser of sycamore trees."

—AMOS 7:14

But of course, Amos was indeed a prophet. In this
part of his story, he's being advised to leave the
country—a sure sign that a prophet has been at work.
What Amos means is that he wasn't an officially
designated prophet, the kind that served at court. He
was simply called by God, from the place where he
was, to speak the truth.

We are sometimes tempted to think that the real
work of Christians is done by the professionals: the
ordained, the consecrated, the church employee. I
know I am, and as a consequence, I can easily settle
into a "let them do it" mentality or end up devaluing
God's activity in my daily life.

God called Amos, a shepherd outside any religious establishment, to speak God's word where he
was. Might he be calling me, as well?

Lord, open my ears to your voice.

July 3

But he said to them, "Unless I see the mark of the nails in his hands, and put my finger in the mark of the nails and my hand in his side, I will not believe."

—JOHN 20:25

Almost everyone has a little voice of doubt, deep within. Each of those small voices has a slightly different timbre and range. For some it is what appears to be unjust suffering. For others it is the great variety of beliefs about God or the failures of church leaders.

My husband says that whenever he is in a big city and is confronted with the sheer multitudes of people around him, he finds it hard to grasp that God is in charge of it all.

I'm sometimes stopped short by love. Could God really love me and care about my problems? Doesn't he have other things to worry about?

Jesus met Thomas's doubts with exactly what he needed. Faith might just mean that we don't understand perfectly but trust that God knows our doubts and has the answers we need if we but approach in honesty, just as Thomas did.

Lord, increase my faith in you.

July 4

As a mother comforts her child,
so I will comfort you;
you shall be comforted in Jerusalem.
—ISAIAH 66:13

Down through the dark hallway it comes, a single sound that makes my heart sink. A cough. Then another. I could see it in her eyes when she got home from school, and I heard it on the edges of her voice.

In the morning, it will be full-blown and there will be no school. And once in a while over the long day or two of recovery, even though she's eight years old—and all grown up if you ask—she'll raise her voice and call out, "I want my mommy!" It's what we want when we're sick. Healing, yes, but comfort, too.

What illness seizes my soul today?

Dare I call out for comfort?

Jesus, heal the sickness in my soul, and give me rest.

July 5

"No one sews a piece of unshrunk cloth on
an old cloak, for the patch pulls away
from the cloak, and a worse tear is made."
—MATTHEW 9:16

As I read the stories of the saints, I am often struck by how many of them spent their lives puzzling, frustrating, and even angering others.

Not that they meant to. Bernadette saw what she saw and couldn't lie about it. Teresa of Ávila simply walked the way of reform in which God was leading her, no matter what some other religious authorities had to say about it. The stories are endless.

God's work always startles. It is always something new. As we try to discern God's will in our lives, we might consider that the strangest answers—those that don't seem to fit our old selves—may sometimes be exactly right.

Lord, help me open my heart to discern the radical ways of your love.

And he said to them, "Why are you afraid, you of little faith?" Then he got up and rebuked the winds and the sea; and there was a dead calm.

—MATTHEW 8:26

The apostles, tossed wildly about on stormy waters, were, not surprisingly, quite frightened.

When we first hear it, Jesus' response might strike us as hard-hearted. There are no promises that he shares our pain.

But he does, and perhaps that's the "faith" he's talking about: knowing him. Perhaps the disciples' faith was small because they didn't really know Jesus—a constant theme of the Gospels, by the way. In the light of the Resurrection and Pentecost, they finally do. They come to understand that knowing Jesus means knowing that he does know our pain and that his care will pull us through.

Jesus, help me to trust in the storm.

July 7

But fornication and impurity of any kind, or greed, must not even be mentioned among you, as is proper among saints. Entirely out of place is obscene, silly, and vulgar talk; but instead, let there be thanksgiving.

—EPHESIANS 5:3–4

I think a lot about time: how much time I have today, how much time is left to me on the planet, how quickly time has passed, and where the time has gone.

Answers: not enough, a lot, way too fast, and I wish I knew.

So time holds a lot of mystery for me, but one thing that's not mysterious is the ability I have to waste it. It's a question of where my head is and what my priorities are. I look at Paul's words in that spirit. Why fill my head and waste my time with matters that bring me down, when I could be filling that same space in a way that brings me closer to God?

Lord, clear my mind, so that I might give it over to you.

July 8

I will remember my covenant with you in
the days of your youth, and I will establish
with you an everlasting covenant.

—Ezekiel 16:60

My youngest son is a toddler now, and sometimes when my daughter and I are with him, I ask her, "Remember when he was tiny and couldn't even hold his head up?"

And she'll say, point blank, "No." Well, the truth is I barely remember myself. The past blends with the present, and one baby blends with the others, and time just keeps moving on.

Sometimes, though, we have to walk intentionally back to the memories to remind ourselves of what this love is all about. The memories of the sleeping baby, the happy first years of marriage and family life, and the carefree days of firm friendship help us refocus on what can still be.

For us, too, it might be a comfort to know that when we feel that we've strayed, God's covenant love for us is ever new. He gazes at us as we look upon that sleeping baby, hearts bursting with love.

Lord, live in my heart, so I might love as you do.

July 9

The heavens are telling the glory of God;
and the firmament proclaims his handiwork.
Day to day pours forth speech,
and night to night declares knowledge.
There is no speech, nor are there words;
their voice is not heard;
yet their voice goes out through all the earth,
and their words to the end of the world.
In the heavens he has set a tent for the sun.

—PSALM 19:1–4

If you've ever really loved, you know how frustrating words of love can be. Those words are so worn out, so overused, so misused, that real love demands something else, something beyond words.

The more important and more profound the thought, the less adequate words are to the task. Only a life, mysterious yet true, will do it justice. That's why these words of the psalmist stop me in my tracks. He knows this, he sees it. God is too much for words. The beauty and wisdom of God's creation expresses that God's nurture and care are beyond the power of words.

Lord, in silence, I am present to you in whatever way you speak to me today.

July 10

For to me, living is Christ and dying is gain.
If I am to live in the flesh, that means fruitful
labor for me; and I do not know which I prefer.

—PHILIPPIANS 1:21–22

I've not yet directly confronted death myself, at least to my knowledge.

But, like anyone with more than forty years behind her, I've had enough minor wake-up calls from my own body; considerations of the rare, but possible, consequences of childbirth; and moments of passing by the scene of an accident minutes after it occurred to have my share of "There but for the grace of God go I" moments.

And when I do contemplate it, like Paul, I'm torn. For, while my faith rejoices in eternal life with Christ, there is no way can I leave my kids, especially now. The thought horrifies me, not for my sake but for theirs. There is much more "fruitful labor" to be done.

It's good because it focuses me on why I'm here in the first place.

Jesus, be glorified through me today.

July 11

Then Jesus said to them, "I ask you, is it
lawful to do good or to do harm on
the sabbath, to save life or to destroy it?"

—LUKE 6:9

❧

My then twelve-year-old daughter had been begging to babysit her little brother. "Okay," I said. "Here's the test. I'm going to the post office. I'll be gone twenty minutes. Entertain him—no television, though." (I knew she would be the one to get more absorbed in television, and Lord knows what would happen.)

I returned, to a crumpled, red face wailing in the window. My daughter, also in tears, said, "He started crying when you left, and wouldn't stop. He wouldn't play with anything."

"You just should have turned on the TV," I said, unthinking. "That would have distracted him."

She looked at me, befuddled. "But you said not to."

As we make our choices during the day, we're called to remember—what's the greater good?

❧

*Lord, help me always serve your children's
deepest needs.*

July 12

The LORD will fulfill his purpose for me;
your steadfast love, O LORD, endures forever.
Do not forsake the work of your hands.
—PSALM 138:8

There was no way I could be with my dying mother. I was nine months pregnant, and she was a six-hour car trip away.

I was kept informed, but it wasn't the same. What frustrated me most was that, as much as those around cared for her, no one shared her faith—our faith. I sensed from what I was being told that there was a spiritual component to my mother's suffering, something that no one there could really deal with, and that I might have been able to assuage, just a little bit. Perhaps.

But faith also tells me that the most important One of all was there, indeed, all the time. I trust that to be true. For my mother. For me. Even when I think I am suffering alone.

Lord, deepen my awareness of your presence here.

July 13

When Abram was ninety-nine years old, the LORD
appeared to Abram, and said to him, "I am God
Almighty; walk before me, and be blameless."

— GENESIS 17:1

To me, faith comes down to completing a sentence.
"If God is God, then . . ."

In other words, if God really exists, then what
does that mean in terms of my life, my purpose, my
destiny, and my fears?

If God is God . . .

Loving God, you are Lord of life.

July 14

O God, you are my God, I seek you,
my soul thirsts for you;
my flesh faints for you,
as in a dry and weary land where there is no water.

—PSALM 63:1

The moment we are born, we confront want and desire. From the comfort and effortless fulfillment of life in the womb, we are thrust into a busy world that doesn't know what we need unless we cry out.

What's more, we find that desires are never truly satisfied. It may take us decades to learn that what we're really trying to find, as we pursue our desires, is a peace that takes hold at our deepest level and never ends.

Has anyone captured it better than St. Augustine, when he wrote, "Our hearts are restless until they rest in Thee, O God"?

Lord, help me turn the frustrations of my life into stirrings to seek my peace in you.

July 15

Now the whole group of those who believed
were of one heart and soul, and no one claimed
private ownership of any possessions, but
everything they owned was held in common.

—ACTS 4:32

❧

My daughter came home from her day at
Catholic school and announced, "Father scared
me today."

"Why?"

"Because at Mass, there was a reading about the
apostles, and it said that they had one heart, and he
said that meant they all thought the same way and did
the same things." She paused. "But I thought we were
special because we were individuals. It scared me."

She was being a little overdramatic about the
"scared" part, but it prompted me to ponder. Does
the prospect of being of one mind and heart with
my brothers and sisters in Christ fill me with joy,
or resistance?

❧

*Jesus, open me to your spirit, so that I may be more
deeply joined to your body.*

July 16

For I, the LORD your God,
hold your right hand;
it is I who say to you, "Do not fear,
I will help you."

—ISAIAH 41:13

In a matter of a day, my toddler son discovered how to be scared. It had to do with a tree that the neighbor children had decorated with a face out of clay, à la *The Wizard of Oz,* and my husband's casual observation of a streetlight going on and off. Somehow, these new things all came together in my son's mind and prompted him to slink around and cling to me, whimpering, "I'm scared."

His previous fearlessness, his effortless trust—all forgotten in light of something new.

Life presents me with new challenges and obstacles all the time. Through it all, can I remember what it means to trust in God?

Lord, I present you with one of my fears. Lead me through it to trust in your care.

July 17

For the LORD is our judge, the LORD is our ruler,
the LORD is our king; he will save us.
—ISAIAH 33:22

I watched a television program last night on child beauty pageants. I found it horrifying. Little bitty girls being primped and practiced, coached to perform and strut down runways by determined, anxious mothers. Just let the little girls go play, I wanted to scream. In fact, I might have.

The worst thing, I think, is this awful lesson being pounded into four-year-old heads: Your value depends on how others judge you.

It's a hard enough lesson to shake, even if your parent never pinned success on the acquisition of a fake silver crown.

Heavenly Father, teach me to look to you, and no one else, for affirmation.

July 18

"For where two or three are gathered in my name,
I am there among them."
—MATTHEW 18:20

As much as I hate to admit it, way too much of the time my prayer is really just about me and my little world. And when I look at the Scriptures and the life of the church, I see how that's just the beginning of prayer.

Prayer is two or three—and even more of us—gathered, in a way, as God's children, giving him praise and thanks. When I go to Mass or when I pray the Liturgy of the Hours on a given day, it's rather breathtaking to realize that I'm joining millions around the world. We are turning our minds and hearts toward God, using exactly the same prayers and Scriptures.

I'm not alone, and—joining my prayer to the entire Body—I don't have to be.

Lord God, I join my prayers to those of all my brothers and sisters.

July 19

For this reason, when I could bear it no longer,
I sent to find out about your faith; I was afraid
that somehow the tempter had tempted you and
that our labor had been in vain.

—1 THESSALONIANS 3:5

Down the midway of the Florida State Fair, temptation was calling two preteen boys. Come play the game, the carneys challenged. Get something cool for hardly any effort.

Such is the call of temptation, in general, isn't it? Prove yourself. Embrace pleasure. Avoid pain at all costs.

There may be some sort of joy in succumbing to temptation, but it is always short-lived, as we learned a mere two days later, when the call came down the stairs.

"Mom, why are the goldfish floating on top of the water?"

Jesus, live in me, and strengthen me against temptation. Help me see what brings me closer to you in the long run.

July 20

Ha! You who hide a plan too deep for the LORD,
whose deeds are in the dark,
and who say, "Who sees us? Who knows us?"
You turn things upside down!

—ISAIAH 29:15–16

One frantic morning years ago, my son was adamant that he felt sick. He didn't look sick to me. "Get in your uniform, and get in the car," I insisted.

He did, but as I was driving out of the carport, he swung the door open so it crashed against a support pole and severely dented the door. This was intense, strange behavior.

He told me later that he wasn't sick at all. There was a kid at school who had been harassing him for days and had told him that this was the day he'd get beaten up. Instead of being honest, though, my son covered it up, and in the process made a lot more trouble for himself.

The truth is hard, but think of the trouble I've generated by avoiding it.

Lord, help me be more honest with you and with others today.

July 21

Evening and morning and at noon
I utter my complaint and moan,
and he will hear my voice.

—PSALM 55:17

My youngest son is definitely a creature of habit. Every sleep period—at nap or at night—must be entered into with stories, in pajamas, and with a drink of water. He wakes up every morning and says the same thing: "Can I have toast and milk in my chair?"

He has his rituals. They give him comfort and a structure from which to safely explore the world or to enter the unknown.

We sometimes resist rituals or set prayer times. We think that life would be so much better if we were free from all that and were spontaneous all the time.

I don't know. For me at least, setting my prayer times and settling into ancient ritual keeps me on the right course, even when my feelings tempt me to skip prayer for today. More important, the tried and tested habits of old give me a safe place from which to enter into the mystery.

Heavenly Father, help me form habits of prayer.

July 22

St. Mary Magdalene

Mary Magdalene went and announced to the
disciples, "I have seen the Lord"; and she
told them that he had said these things to her.

—JOHN 20:18

Emerging from all the legends and fiction about her, Mary Magdalene stands here as simply a faithful, loving, courageous disciple.

There seemed to be no point in remaining, in waiting, or in returning to that tomb. What did this Jesus have to do with anything anymore?

Faithful and trusting, even in mystery, Mary found out.

Lord God, help me be faithful as Mary Magdalene was, in a world that has abandoned you.

July 23

Is it nothing to you, all you who pass by?
Look and see
if there is any sorrow like my sorrow.
—Lamentations 1:12

I was pouring out my latest troubles to my friend. Then I stopped, looked at her, and thought, *Here we have me, with my supposedly broken heart, and her with a recently deceased parent, breast cancer, and various serious personal challenges she has endured with grace.*

"I'm sorry," I said. "This is stupid. It's nothing. I should just get over it." My friend's eyes brimmed with sympathy. "Pain is pain," she said. "The source doesn't matter. It's pain and it hurts."

Then she lifted her wineglass, tipped it back, and drained it. "But you're right," she added. "You should get over it. And soon."

Yes, ma'am.

Loving God, I know you are with me in my pain.
Help me endure and pass to the other side.

July 24

"When you are praying, do not heap up empty
phrases as the Gentiles do; for they think that
they will be heard because of their many words."
—MATTHEW 6:7

I've often joined in monastic prayer, and I've wit-
nessed this many times:

We enter into a part of the prayer that is respon-
sorial in nature. The presider says: "The Lord be with
you." Visitors to the monastery respond immediately:
"And also with you."

Literally five seconds later, here come the monks.
"And also with you."

Imagine that. Actually taking your time to pray!

Jesus, slow me down so that I might hear your voice.

Do you not know that in a race the runners all compete, but only one receives the prize? Run in such a way that you may win it. Athletes exercise self-control in all things; they do it to receive a perishable wreath, but we an imperishable one.

—1 CORINTHIANS 9:24–25

When my daughter was about three, we attended a minor-league baseball game. After the game, children were allowed on the field to run the bases. We all watched in astonishment as little pigtailed Katie's legs churned like mad, taking her single-mindedly to her goal.

Until, right before home plate, her sandals got the best of her and—*splat*—down she went.

In tears, she let me escort her to the bathroom, but not before an elderly gentleman stopped and handed her a dollar. Afterward, I asked her if she knew why she'd received the dollar from the man.

"Because I was the winner," she sniffed.

Am I sitting still, or am I running toward Jesus with all my strength?

Jesus, keep my eyes fixed on you.

July 26

Anxiety weighs down the human heart,
but a good word cheers it up.
—PROVERBS 12:25

The woman standing directly ahead of me in line at the pharmacy was in her early forties. Casually dressed, she nervously tapped her purchase against her leg. When it was her turn, she thrust the item—a pregnancy test—at the cashier and asked, "Do you have a restroom I could use?"

Waving aside the offer of a bag, the woman headed in the direction of the restroom. She had no time to waste. For whatever reason, she had to know.

There is nothing that makes us more anxious than the unknown, I thought as I offered a quick prayer for that woman. Let her find peace, I prayed. Let the rest of us find it, too.

Lord, there is an area of life that worries me. I offer it to you. Your will be done.

July 27

You show me the path of life.
In your presence there is fullness of joy;
in your right hand are pleasures forevermore.
—PSALM 16:11

I have reached the conclusion that my toddler son is extremely neurotic. Or something.

Especially in regard to clothes. If he's sitting in his car seat and his shirt gets hiked up in the back, it's an occasion for a fit that will not cease until the shirt is pulled back down. If he spills a drop or two of milk or juice on his shirt, it must be changed. Which is a problem, since he is also very fond of brushing his teeth "all by myself."

The point is, what seem to me like the most minor incidents can disrupt his happy mood. Why, I wonder, let go of joy for such silly reasons?

Good question.

Lord God, help me see through the annoyances of my day to the joy of your constant love.

I have loved you with an everlasting love;
therefore I have continued my faithfulness to you.
—JEREMIAH 31:3

At a point in my life when I was feeling a bit at sea, I took my daughter to the beach. I was unhappy in my job, yearning for something different, afraid to take steps in that direction, and wondering, in general, why I had been put here.

I watched my daughter play. She hadn't asked to come to the beach that day. I'd just picked her up and brought her. I knew she could use the elements around her—sea and sand, shells and seaweed—to create a contented space.

I knew she could. I wouldn't have brought her here if I didn't.

Loving God, you have brought me to the place I am now. Guide me to find peace in the present.

July 29

Lord, hear my voice!
Let your ears be attentive
to the voice of my supplications!

—PSALM 130:2

When my middle son was quite young, he once ended his nighttime prayers by mumbling, "For Beethoven." Startled, I asked him why he was praying for Beethoven.

In utter seriousness, he replied, "So he'll get his hearing back."

Sometimes my prayer is way too measured, too concerned with what's proper and with what makes sense theologically. I think I might be missing something.

Heavenly Father, I offer you the deepest prayers of my heart, unconcerned with how silly or strange they may sound.

July 30

"Why do you call me 'Lord, Lord,' and do
not do what I tell you? I will show you
what someone is like who comes to me,
hears my words, and acts on them."

—LUKE 6:46–47

After more than two decades of mothering, I admit that I've come to be a little suspicious. Perhaps too suspicious, especially since the phrase that rouses my suspicion most quickly is "I love you, Mom."

I guess it started when my oldest sons were quite small. One would observe the other being punished and would immediately appear with a winning smile, saying, "I wuv you." Sweet.

And as they got older, the phrase was usually uttered around the same time some chores were not being done, prompting me to scowl. "If you really loved me, you'd do what I say."

Ah, yes. Mirror, please?

Jesus, I love you. Live in me today, and bring my words and my deeds into a single movement of love toward you.

July 31

St. Ignatius of Loyola

"So therefore, none of you can become my disciple
if you do not give up all your possessions."

—Luke 14:33

St. Ignatius gave it all up at midlife. He turned from the prospect of earthly wealth and glory to a life dedicated to serving God.

He wrote a prayer that puts this decision into words, a prayer that is centered on the "possession" I most value:

> Take, Lord, and receive all my liberty,
> my memory, my understanding
> and my entire will,
> All that I have and possess.
>
> Thou has given all to me.
> To Thee, O Lord, I return it.

Lord, you have given me everything. I hand my most prized possessions over to you in love and hope.

August

August 1

As they were gathering in Galilee, Jesus said
to them, "The Son of Man is going to be
betrayed into human hands, and they will
kill him, and on the third day he will be
raised." And they were greatly distressed.

—MATTHEW 17:22–23

I admit that far too often, I can identify with Jesus'
apostles here. They have just heard Jesus predict
his passion. He will be killed, he says, and then raised
on the third day.

But wait—he says he will be raised. Why are they
distressed? Because they did not understand, I suppose. They couldn't—it was too startling to envision.
They hadn't encountered the risen Jesus yet.

And so it is with me. When I'm gripped with a
fear of death, I refocus. I consider the Resurrection.
Do I believe this really happened? Yes, I do. So what's
the problem?

Perhaps, like the apostles, for it all to be real, I
need to meet the living, risen Christ. Again.

Jesus, may I embrace the new life you offer me.

August 2

And God is able to provide you with every
blessing in abundance, so that by always
having enough of everything, you may share
abundantly in every good work.

—2 CORINTHIANS 9:8

It's not unusual for new parents to study their
freshly hatched bundle of joy in wonder, asking
themselves, "How did we do this?"

It's also not unusual for new parents to be seized
by fear the very next moment: "How are we ever going
to do this?"

It can seem an impossible task to raise an emotionally healthy, spiritually grounded child in this
wrecked world, especially when you're not even sure
which side of the diaper goes up.

Paul tells us what is good to hear then and now:
God knows what he's doing. He's placed us here, and
through his grace we can work with him to do good,
no matter what the situation, how daunting the task,
or how unworthy we feel.

*Lord, today I place a difficult part of my life before
you. Help me receive your strengthening grace.*

August 3

Restore to me the joy of your salvation,
and sustain in me a willing spirit.
—PSALM 51:12

There is a certain sadness that some people cling to like a drug. It's a sadness that can turn to anger and then bitterness. It's the sadness that results when we don't accept God's forgiveness for sins.

Remorse is good. Contrition, repentance, and sorrow for sin are all healthy responses to the choices that have hurt others and taken us away from God. But in our journey to holiness, we can't stop with remorse. God calls us to take another step forward, toward his forgiveness and the promise of wholeness.

What part of my life can I let God renew today?

Lord, I take that next step. Let your love create that clean heart I so desire.

August 4

"What woman having ten silver coins, if she loses
one of them, does not light a lamp, sweep the
house, and search carefully until she finds it?"

—LUKE 15:8

A baby, at age one year, is an expert in emptying
things. He can pull a shelf's worth of books or
CDs onto the floor while my back is turned. He does
enjoy his actual toys, but only when they're piled up
in a big plastic container so that he can spend several
blissful minutes simply pulling them out, one by one.

And then move on. For you see, making a mess
comes naturally to the baby. Restoring order does not.

God's activity is, in a way, a constant invitation
for us to cooperate with him in restoring order to
our world and our lives. He created each of us in his
image, to be his own beloved for eternity. When any
of us strays or is lost, the order of creation is disturbed
and, as Jesus tells us, God will do all he can to restore
it. To restore us.

*Loving God, take the parts of my life that are lost,
and restore them in your love.*

August 5

We always give thanks to God for all of you
and mention you in our prayers, constantly
remembering before our God and Father your
work of faith and labor of love and steadfastness
of hope in our Lord Jesus Christ.

—1 Thessalonians 1:2–3

For whose witness and faith should I thank God?
I can thank God for my parents, who brought
me to the waters of baptism. Also, for the Southern
Baptist friend in the eighth grade who asked me a million "whys" about being Catholic and wouldn't take "I
don't know" for an answer. For my husband and my
children. And for saints, across space and time, who
teach me how to live with joy.

In the end, in all honesty, truth and joy, I join
my own prayer across twenty centuries and echo the
words of Paul, thanking God and praying for all I
have met on this journey.

*Lord, today I thank you for those who have sacrificed
so that I might know you.*

"Why have you brought us up out of Egypt, to bring us to this wretched place? It is no place for grain, or figs, or vines, or pomegranates; and there is no water to drink."

—NUMBERS 20:5

Isn't it odd how sometimes the place we absolutely knew was the place for us—where God wants us to be—ends up being a little more complicated? We wonder, has God changed his mind, or does he want us to be miserable?

It's a difficult situation to be in, as the Israelites discovered in the desert. With patience and an open heart—to the needs of others, not just our own—God's will can become clear again.

Until the next time, at least.

Lord, when I begin to feel burned-out, help me seek your loving presence wherever I am.

August 7

"Be on your guard! If another disciple sins, you must rebuke the offender, and if there is repentance, you must forgive. And if the same person sins against you seven times a day, and turns back to you seven times and says, 'I repent,' you must forgive."

—LUKE 17:3–4

The two brothers had been picking on each other for hours before the final explosion occurred. The gory details are irrelevant, just the final scene in which the mother attempted closure.

"Say you're sorry!" she ordered, and she was obeyed grudgingly and with total insincerity. She knew it was the best she could do at the time, and sometimes temporary, superficial peace will just have to do.

Offering an insincere apology is one thing, but how often is our offer of forgiveness just as shallow? How many times do we say, "Sure, I forgive you," while secretly storing away the offense in the depth of our hearts as a weapon to be drawn out later?

What kind of forgiveness is that?

Jesus, help me extend your authentic peace and forgiveness to others.

August 8

So Jesus said to them, "Very truly, I tell you,
unless you eat the flesh of the Son of Man
and drink his blood, you have no life in you."

—JOHN 6:53

✤

When I'm hungry, I feel empty and edgy. I feel
weakened, distracted, and as if something's
missing.

In other words, I feel less than fully alive.

And when I feel my spiritual life leaching away . . .
who can nourish me?

✤

*Jesus, I come to you in Eucharist, yearning for
your life.*

August 9

You foolish Galatians! Who has bewitched you?
It was before your eyes that Jesus Christ was
publicly exhibited as crucified!

—GALATIANS 3:1

As disciples of Jesus, some of us struggle with
the issue of criticism. Isn't it impolite to draw
attention to another's errors? Doesn't it show a lack
of charity to point out how wrong someone is? And
doesn't it just make us uncomfortable, besides?

As Paul shows us here, though, telling it like it
is can be an important element of Christian witness.
After all, how is letting another continue down a dangerous path a loving act?

*Lord Jesus, help me discern how to be truthful at all
times, and in charity.*

August 10

Be still before the LORD, and wait patiently for him;
do not fret over those who prosper in their way,
over those who carry out evil devices.

—PSALM 37:7

I think that one of the most difficult concepts for a child to learn is "wait." They just don't get it. If what's coming is so great, why must they wait? Why not now?

I write this just as my little son has come to my desk, demanding a new paper napkin to replace the one he's shredded in the midst of his mysterious, private game. He doesn't want to wait. To him, "wait" is just the same as "no."

Is he really unique, though? Is he the only one who feels this way? Or at times do I, as well, find it impossible to wait?

Lord, give me patience and the wisdom to find you in the waiting.

August 11

ST. CLARE OF ASSISI

I want to know Christ and the power of his
resurrection and the sharing of his sufferings
by becoming like him in his death.
—PHILIPPIANS 3:10

It may surprise us to learn that St. Clare, among other things, is the patron saint of television. Why? The story goes that on Christmas, near death, unable to attend Mass, she saw the Mass before her, as if she were there. Television can be marvelous, of course, but it obviously needs a patron saint.

Clare sought, above all, to conform her life to Christ, as Paul says we should all do.

But it's a good question to ask: What impact does television have on my own sense of whom I should be like? To whom am I really trying to conform my life?

Heavenly Father, help me reflect on the power of media in my life and on my sense of who I'm called to be. St. Clare, pray for us.

August 12

Do not be deceived; God is not mocked, for you
reap whatever you sow. If you sow to your own
flesh, you will reap corruption from the flesh; but
if you sow to the Spirit, you will reap eternal life
from the Spirit. So let us not grow weary in doing
what is right, for we will reap at harvesttime, if
we do not give up.

—GALATIANS 6:7–9

I admit it. My library fines had built up to the point
that I couldn't check out books anymore! No
problem. I would just rely on my daughter's card. I
would avoid parting with my money and facing the
wrath of the librarian.

Until the day that, for work purposes, I had to
use interlibrary loan. There was no way around it, and
university archival libraries aren't going to send mate-
rials to a twelve-year-old's account.

It's very hard to avoid the wages of sin forever.
Not that you should even try.

*Loving God, be with me as I confront my weaknesses
and find strength in you.*

August 13

And he said, "Hear my words:
When there are prophets among you,
I the LORD make myself known to them in visions;
I speak to them in dreams."

—NUMBERS 12:6

Ienvy people who have peaceful, soothing
dreams. I don't think I've ever had a dream like
that in my life. The dreams I remember are full of
anxiety, usually centered on the theme of having
to be somewhere or do something, with countless
obstacles along the way.

Don't tell me God doesn't speak to us through
dreams anymore. I think I can learn a lot about my
own life, in reflecting on my dreams.

*Lord of wisdom, teach me as I reflect on my
own dreams.*

August 14

"As for what was sown among thorns, this
is the one who hears the word, but the
cares of the world and the lure of wealth
choke the word, and it yields nothing."

—MATTHEW 13:22

Afflicted with a headache one night, I pondered pain. At least 95 percent of my body didn't hurt. Why was it I only felt the part that did? Why did that overwhelm everything else?

So I tried something. I concentrated my full attention on a part of my body that didn't hurt: my hand. And lo and behold, for the seconds that I was able to maintain my concentration, I didn't "feel" the pain in my head. It was kind of strange.

When one part of my life is problematic, why does that overwhelm the rest? Why does it threaten to uproot me from my confidence in God's love and presence?

Jesus, through life's pain, may I stay focused on you.

August 15

ASSUMPTION

It is sown a physical body, it is raised a spiritual
body. If there is a physical body, there is also a
spiritual body.

—1 CORINTHIANS 15:44

Since conception, my body has changed dramati-
cally. What began as a single cell is now a bit larger
than that. The soft skin of infancy is getting worn.
Reading glasses are becoming a necessity. I wonder as
I watch elderly women walk past me in the grocery
store, in a few decades, who will I be?

I will be the same person, in a body that so mysteriously changes but is somehow still me and will,
God promises, remain so for eternity. One more great
change will take place, one that I cannot even imagine, but I will remain myself, only whole.

This is what we celebrate today, what God has
shared with Mary: eternal life of our whole selves.
There is nothing to fear, for life is the victor!

Lord, thank you for the gift of eternal life.
Hail Mary . . .

August 16

Humble yourselves therefore under the
mighty hand of God, so that he may
exalt you in due time. Cast all your anxiety
on him, because he cares for you.

—1 Peter 5:6–7

Each writer has his or her own excuses for difficulties, and mine is a strange kind of perfectionism (which is totally absent in the rest of my life, like
housekeeping). Sometimes it's hard for me to simply
get the words down and commit to them because I
want them to be perfect; but I know they're not, and
I don't want to put anything out there that's less than
perfect.

I do, indeed, want my words to be as perfect as
possible in expressing the truth I'm trying to write
about. But, also, I'm just plain proud.

Is my perfectionism a way of striving for excellence, or is it a battle against the truth that I'm not
God?

*God of all, thank you for my life, in all its
imperfections.*

August 17

"If you love those who love you, what credit is that to you? For even sinners love those who love them. If you do good to those who do good to you, what credit is that to you? For even sinners do the same."

—LUKE 6:32–33

This one always hits me like a ton of bricks. This is what it means to let Jesus live in me.

No excuses. Am I disciple, or not?

Jesus, fill me with your love and the strength to share it.

August 18

Many Samaritans from that city believed
in him because of the woman's testimony,
"He told me everything I have ever done."

—JOHN 4:39

My daughter is in this awkward, preteen stage in which she is obviously trying to figure out how to be in the world. And because she's naturally dramatic, she tends to be dramatic about it. She takes on the traits of whoever she's decided to be that day— the high-school girls, one of her friends, a character in a movie, even me—and she exaggerates it to the point where it's as if she's playing a part.

It irritates me, and I just want to tell her to be herself. Sometimes I do. But then I realize she probably doesn't know who that is yet.

Like the rest of us, she needs to learn to trust Jesus and let him tell her all he knows about her. Only then can she learn to live as herself.

Lord, you have put me here for a reason. Help me discern who I am in this world you made.

August 19

Take my instruction instead of silver,
and knowledge rather than choice gold;
for wisdom is better than jewels,
and all that you may desire cannot
compare with her.

—PROVERBS 8:10–11

This is worth pondering, and frequently. Do I believe this? Really?

What compromises have I made in pursuit of financial security or success? What price have I paid? And what am I willing to pay or sacrifice in order to have God's instructions, knowledge, and wisdom?

Lord of wisdom, help me honestly discern whom I really serve.

August 20

O Lord, how manifold are your works!
In wisdom you have made them all;
the earth is full of your creatures.
—Psalm 104:24

It was a typical backseat battle. There wasn't enough room, and the older brother was making it worse by sitting on his knees, taking more space than he deserved. His then five-year-old sister protested. "Legs aren't for sittin'! Bottoms are for sittin'!"

Natural law—in which everything created has a purpose and proper use, intended by God—out of the mouths of babes. It is amazing and mysterious to look around me and realize that every corner, every speck of creation came from the hand of God, and nothing is accidental. It is pure gift, all of it, to be treasured and cared for . . .

. . . and used properly, as even a little one can tell you.

God of the universe, may I move in this creation of yours in a way that respects your intentions and gives you glory.

August 21

Oh, that I had one to hear me!
(Here is my signature! let the Almighty answer me!)
—JOB 31:35

One of the most seriously wrongheaded aphorisms ever dreamt up just might be "the patience of Job." For the fact is, Job was not patient. His friends, advising him in his troubles, told him to be patient and just accept the fact that, according to the wisdom of the time, he must have done something really wrong to bring on himself such punishment as he was suffering.

But he didn't. He justified himself, he questioned, and ultimately he demanded an answer from God: *Why is this happening to me?*

And the amazing thing is, God answered. He didn't answer the compliant friends. He spoke from the whirlwind and responded to the bold, frustrated questions of Job.

Lord, I give you my deepest questions and fears.
Answer me.

August 22

[Love] does not insist on its own way;
it is not irritable or resentful.
—1 Corinthians 13:5

My oldest son was in a dilemma. He was having trouble trying to figure out how he should act toward a young woman who'd treated him badly but who was obviously troubled. It was a yo-yo kind of situation, and everything my son was trying to do seemed to make it worse.

"But I care about her," he said. "I want her to be happy." He finally understood that maybe the best thing to do would be to step back. He was reluctant to do so because he thought it would make him look bad. But he knew that the best thing was to point her in a more helpful direction, pray for her, and set aside his own self-interest—in this case, his ego.

Love is all these things. Love is also hard.

Lord, help me discern if my actions are really loving in the long run.

August 23

For everything there is a season, and a
time for every matter under heaven:
a time to be born, and a time to die;
a time to plant, and a time to pluck up
what is planted.

—ECCLESIASTES 3:1–2

A few months after my mother passed away, when I was on a summer visit home, my father asked me to go through her things, take what I wanted, and sort the rest for donation to charity. He would be gone for the day while I did this. And I didn't mind doing it.

My oldest son, though, was offended. "How can you do that?" he asked, hurt, almost as if I were going through his possessions.

It wasn't easy, but it had to be done because, like it or not, time moves on. And faith keeps my eyes fixed on the point at which there will be no time, and no pain of its passing, only joy.

Lord, I put my hope in eternal life with you.

August 24

But Jonah set out to flee to Tarshish from the presence of the LORD. He went down to Joppa and found a ship going to Tarshish; so he paid his fare and went on board, to go with them to Tarshish, away from the presence of the LORD.

—JONAH 1:3

My toddler son goes to a sitter a few mornings a week, while I work. On some days, when there's more work than usual to be done, he stays all day. He knows these days because he sees his bag with his blanket and stuffed monkey waiting by the steps.

Which he immediately tries to hide, reasoning that if the bag's gone, he won't have to nap at Peggy's. Sorry. It doesn't work that way. Some things you just can't avoid.

I can't rearrange my life or hide parts of it, thinking that by doing so I can keep God away. Jonah discovered that, and so have I, many times.

Loving God, I welcome your presence in all parts of my life.

August 25

Making a whip of cords, he drove all of them
out of the temple, both the sheep and the cattle.
He also poured out the coins of the money
changers and overturned their tables. He told
those who were selling the doves, "Take these
things out of here! Stop making my Father's
house a marketplace!"

—JOHN 2:15–16

I make a living writing about religion, and it gnaws
at my conscience, quite honestly. My husband says,
"Well, they're either going to give their money to the
Walton family (as in Wal-Mart) or us, so they might
as well give it to us."

Funny. But still, I've never been able to rest easy
with it. And I hope I never will, not in my career, nor
in the rest of the way I live out my faith, either. The
profit motive isn't always about money, you know.

Jesus, I give you my faith. Clear it of self-interested
motives, and root me in love and sacrifice.

August 26

Though they knew God, they did not honor him as
God or give thanks to him, but they became futile
in their thinking, and their senseless minds were
darkened. Claiming to be wise, they became fools.

—ROMANS 1:21–22

My son, ordered to cooperate with his younger
sister's request to play, complied. And very
cleverly, I must say, complied in a way that sent her
running to me five minutes later, saying, "David's
mean. I don't want to play with him anymore."

Looks like he got what he wanted.

In the same way, if we decide to keep God at a
distance, we might be surprised someday to discover
the consequences. God's always near, but the more we
turn and push away, the less able we are to recognize
the gift of that presence.

*Lord, you love faithfully, even if I try to push you
away. Help me open every corner of my life to you.*

August 27

St. Monica

I wait for the LORD, my soul waits,
and in his word I hope;
my soul waits for the Lord.
—PSALM 130:5–6

For a long time, I wasn't too keen on St. Monica, the mother of St. Augustine, who was so intent on his salvation that she followed him across the sea from North Africa to Italy. She struck me as rather a nag, perhaps a bit obsessed. *Let go, woman,* I thought. *Just let your son be.*

Then my oldest son started having a life. And then the next one did, too. They were living their lives away from my sight. No, I didn't follow them, as Monica followed Augustine, and neither have I directed their personal lives. Much.

But I have felt tenacious love that has not weakened one bit by distance. And I have sought to respond to that, not by worrying or nagging (much) but mostly through what Monica's witness leads me to: prayer.

Loving Father, I put those whom I love in your hands. Guide and protect them.

August 28

St. Augustine of Hippo

My soul yearns for you in the night,
my spirit within me earnestly seeks you.
—Isaiah 26:9

When I read St. Augustine's *Confessions,* I'm always amazed that something written sixteen hundred years ago can still be so pertinent. A man seeks happiness through the pleasures of the flesh, through entertainment, and through material success. He's pushed into schooling and a profession by his parents. He gets involved in a trendy spiritual movement.

And all of it leaves him unsatisfied and still yearning.

What Augustine tells me through the centuries is still so true: What I want is a happiness that never ends and a love that is total and eternal. Why in the world am I looking for the eternal among things that will break, fail, and die?

One of Augustine's most famous phrases: "Our hearts are restless until they rest in you, O Lord."

Eternal God, direct my heart to your faithful love.

August 29

BEHEADING OF JOHN THE BAPTIST

Herod feared John, knowing that he was a
righteous and holy man, and he protected
him. When he heard him, he was greatly
perplexed; and yet he liked to listen to him.

—MARK 6:20

When a difficult moral decision is before me, I am
often tempted to work through the same set of of
excuses. I know what the right thing to do is. I think the
world would be a better place if we all lived according
to that right thing. I'd be happier, too. But I just can't do
that right thing now. Next time, sure. But not now.

Like Herod, we are a bit confused by truth. We can't
help but recognize the power of the truth, but it frightens
us. But then the moment comes when we're challenged
to apply it to our own lives, and the temptation rises, fast
and furious, to lock up truth and keep it in custody. It's
still there. We can pay ourselves the compliment of not
having ignored it completely. But apply it to the choices
we must make today? Maybe next time.

*Lord, I know the truth of your love and call brings
me joy. Help me bring that loving truth into every
moment of my daily life.*

We have this hope, a sure and
steadfast anchor of the soul.

—HEBREWS 6:19

Quite often, the only thing that gets my toddler son to sleep is the promise of what awaits him when he wakes up.

When he wakes up, he'll have cinnamon toast (an inexplicably big thrill). When he wakes up from his nap, his big sister will be home from school to play with him. These, it seems, make the inconvenience of sleep worthwhile.

So it is with us. Would that naps were our greatest challenges. Sometimes the rewards of discipleship are hard, if not impossible, to discern in the short term. Sometimes all we have is God's promise of the joys that await us, after the pain is done and morning has come.

Jesus, keep my eyes on the joy you have promised.

August 31

You are indeed my rock and my fortress;
for your name's sake lead me and guide me.

—PSALM 31:3

I do a lot of public speaking. As I get into the flow of a talk, I invariably find myself searching for a friendly face—someone who's nodding at my points or smiling or just looking terribly interested.

That person then becomes my anchor, the rock whose pleasant face assures me that I'm not wasting my time.

That's okay to do in that particular context, but I must be careful not to expand the habit into the rest of life. I can't depend on the approval of others in order to feel secure. Only God can be that kind of anchor for me.

❧

Lord, you are my rock. Give me strength today.

September

September 1

Your boasting is not a good thing. Do you not know
that a little yeast leavens the whole batch of dough?
—1 Corinthians 5:6

When I was a teenager, I used to drive myself to
the library on Saturday afternoons and park
my 1973 Dodge Coronet in the self-policing pay lot.
One day I bragged to my father that I'd figured out
the money collector's schedule, and, by planning my
library time accordingly, I could avoid paying.

Unimpressed, my father spoke simply as he closed
the refrigerator door and walked out of the kitchen.
"Then you are a thief."

The memory still gives me a chill, killing temptation just as cold water takes the life out of yeast.
Are there times in our lives in which we, like the
Corinthians to whom St. Paul wrote, confuse our
freedom in Christ with a license to sin?

*Lord, be with me as I search my conscience and
welcome your forgiveness.*

September 2

Let no one despise your youth, but set
the believers an example in speech and
conduct, in love, in faith, in purity.
—1 TIMOTHY 4:12

Who can teach us about faith? Isn't it odd that so much of the time, it's the most unlikely characters?

Our culture tempts us constantly to seek wisdom only from its self-defined best and brightest, successful, and mainstream. That doesn't seem to be the Christian way, which, when you think about it, makes sense for a people who see God's love revealed in his broken body on a cross.

Loving God, open my heart to your ways in the world, no matter how strange they may seem to me at first.

September 3

"But as for that in the good soil, these are
the ones who, when they hear the word,
hold it fast in an honest and good heart,
and bear fruit with patient endurance."

—LUKE 8:15

Listening to Jesus tell the parable of the sower, we quite naturally fit ourselves and those we know into the categories Jesus presents. Most of us would say that our lives at one time or another have been composed of every kind of soil that Jesus describes.

When we search our hearts for our place in Jesus' scenario, we tend to focus on the hard, infertile, and rocky times. It is important to do this, but perhaps it's even more helpful to consider those moments when we've really allowed God's grace to take root. What was going on? What frame of mind made our spirits so fertile and open? What do we need to let go of in order to be fruitful once again?

Lord, give me the grace to be unafraid of the bountiful fruit you want to grow in my life.

September 4

"Indeed, God did not send the Son into the world
to condemn the world, but in order that the
world might be saved through him."

—JOHN 3:17

My oldest son had trouble adjusting to college
life. He found his niche, certainly, and it was
a fruitful one, a great job related to his career goals.
The problem was that rather essential aspect of college
called classes. He didn't take to them. He made mistakes. He got depressed and condemned himself to
"failure."

Too many of us allow ourselves to be defined by
our mistakes and sins, believing that this must be the
identity borne by us always.

It's just not so. No matter what we've done, the
good news Jesus brings is that God forgives, that God
gives us the grace to start over, and that the only identity God gives us is that of his own beloved child.

Loving God, I know I am not my mistakes.
Thank you for the grace to start over.

September 5

I can do all things through him who strengthens me.
—PHILIPPIANS 4:13

It was one of the biggest things I had ever seen: a Saturn V rocket laid out at the Kennedy Space Center in Florida. I couldn't believe that it actually got off the ground. I couldn't believe that human beings had figured out how to do this. Who could even think about it without giving up and saying, "Impossible"?

And I had to think, too, about all the far smaller challenges we face every day that cause us to throw up our hands and say, "I can't! It's impossible!" Too hard to forgive, too hard to endure, too hard to love.

Really?

Jesus, fill me with the possibilities of your love.

September 6

Again Jesus spoke to them, saying, "I am the light
of the world. Whoever follows me will never
walk in darkness but will have the light of life."

—JOHN 8:12

L ife is pretty good right now, all things considered.
Who needs a savior, anyway?
Who?

*Jesus, help me examine my heart. Forgive me for the
times I live as though I don't need your light.*

September 7

"You have heard that it was said, 'An eye for an
eye and a tooth for a tooth.' But I say to you,
Do not resist an evildoer. But if anyone strikes
you on the right cheek, turn the other also."

—MATTHEW 5:38–39

I told my little son to clean his plate. He looked at
me quizzically, then picked up his napkin and
obediently started wiping down his plate, still half-
filled with food. I bought him a new shirt, telling him
it would be good to eat out in. We went to a restaurant,
ate, and left. He cried, saying, "This shirt for eatin'
out! I wanna eat outside!"

Taking words too literally can have its pitfalls.

Of course, taking words not literally enough can
have a whole other set of pitfalls, as we learn when we
do this with Jesus, especially when we try to explain
away his harder words.

*Lord Jesus, guide me as I commit my heart more
deeply to your words.*

September 8

BIRTH OF MARY

But I trusted in your steadfast love;
my heart shall rejoice in your salvation.
I will sing to the LORD,
because he has dealt bountifully with me.
—PSALM 13:5–6

Through the life of Mary, I see so clearly, once again, God's ways. The unknown girl, born far away from earthly importance, wearing no crowns, holding no power—she is the one through whom God gave the world its Savior.

What other wonders is God working right now, through his humble, joyful ones? Am I even paying attention?

Loving God, open my eyes to your presence in all people.

September 9

"No slave can serve two masters; for a slave
will either hate the one and love the other,
or be devoted to the one and despise the
other. You cannot serve God and wealth."

—LUKE 16:13

I was never a rabid lottery player, but I did play. And I did contemplate the problems that the winnings would solve and the pleasures they would bring. In the Scriptures, Jesus warns us that the desire for money is an obstacle to a deeper relationship with God. I thought I could handle it.

Until the day it hit me that, even though my odds for winning were ridiculously bad, perhaps it was true that just buying a ticket, wishing, and hoping were little acts of faithlessness.

Did I believe Jesus or not?

Lord, I am sorry for turning from the truth of your word, even in small ways.

September 10

When he saw the crowds, he had compassion
for them, because they were harassed
and helpless, like sheep without a shepherd.
—MATTHEW 9:36

I was teaching high school in Florida, when one day,
a circus train (really) derailed a block away from
our school.

Of course, the townspeople filled the roads as
they came to gawk. And then a helicopter from a television station, coming to film the scene, crashed in
our soccer field. It was a busy day.

The world is filled with suffering, and, thanks
to the media, it's available for our viewing twenty-
four hours a day. What's our response? Is it all just
a sick form of entertainment, or does it fill us with
the compassion of Jesus, a compassion that moves us
to love?

*Jesus, fill me with your compassion for the suffering
of others and the courage to act on it.*

September 11

"Blessed are you who weep now,
for you will laugh."
—LUKE 6:21

✧

Those images will never leave us. We sat, stunned, in front of our televisions, seeing the unthinkable happen over and over again as the footage replayed and the images were seared into our souls.

One plane, then another. Still more. Buildings in flames, then, unbelievably, collapsing. A hell of flames and choking dust and debris. Worst of all, bodies falling. Our imaginations not allowing us to stop picturing the mothers clutching their babies, teachers holding fast to their young students; nor could we stop hearing the brave calls home with last words of love.

To believe that one day all this weeping could ever be overwhelmed by joy would require answering a radical, and some might say bizarre, promise.

Jesus knows the weeping. And nevertheless, he promises.

✧

Lord, today we pray for all the victims of violence over the past year. We pray for peace.

September 12

Come now, you who say, "Today or tomorrow
we will go to such and such a town and spend a
year there, doing business and making money."
Yet you do not even know what tomorrow will
bring. What is your life? For you are a mist that
appears for a little while and then vanishes.

—JAMES 4:13–14

I sat in the bleachers on a muggy, fall Florida night,
watching a high-school football game. My daughter
was rather small at the time, and I was distracted from
the action on the field by her adventures. In fact, most
of the time, I missed the big plays, alerted afterward
by the roar of the crowd.

The first few times this happened, the same
strange thought popped into my head: I'd see it on
instant replay.

Well, no. Television had spoiled me. Perhaps it
had even worked to deceive me. This is life. There are
no instant replays.

*Lord, teach me to treasure the gift of every moment
that you give me.*

"God is spirit, and those who worship him
must worship in spirit and truth."

—JOHN 4:24

Ionce wrote a snide piece about the preaching
in Catholic churches, claiming that I'd probably
heard three good homilies over the past couple of
years, tops.

A few weeks later, a friend told me that the pastor
had commented on my piece, remarking that he had
presided over perhaps three good worship assemblies
over the past couple of years, tops. Ouch.

When I go to Mass, I might consider spend-
ing more time actually worshipping rather than
criticizing.

*God of all, move me to true worship, and help me set
my ego aside.*

September 14

"Just so, I tell you, there will be more joy in heaven over one sinner who repents than over ninety-nine righteous persons who need no repentance."

—LUKE 15:7

When I taught high-school religion, it was very common for a discussion on morality to end this way: Someone would lean back and pose what he or she felt was just the most killer question of all—"So, someone who (fill in the blank) is going straight to hell?"

The implication being that if the answer is no—which of course it is, most of the time—then there's really nothing wrong with the act or attitude in question.

There is so much more to it, isn't there? When a loving, gracious, wonderful God is the center of your life, sin becomes much more than rules and punishment. It's about a whole other level of heartbreak and mercy.

Loving Father, help me see the damage my sin is doing to my life and to your hopes for me.

September 15

OUR LADY OF SORROWS

Hear the voice of my supplication,
as I cry to you for help,
as I lift up my hands
toward your most holy sanctuary.

—PSALM 28:2

Sickness is a place," the writer Flannery O'Connor once said. She spoke from experience: Her place of residence was called lupus, and it killed her when she was only thirty-nine.

What O'Connor said about sickness can be said of any kind of deep sorrow. Empathize all we can, we still do not know sorrow until we have visited that place and walked among its questions, its pain, and its solitude.

But are we really so alone there? Or will we find Mary, whose heart was pierced? Like her, when we lift our hands and our voices to the holy place of God's love, we find the comfort that we are promised.

Lord, I bring you the parts of my life that bring me sadness. Assure me of your presence, even in the midst of my pain.

September 16

"And now, Lord, look at their threats, and grant
to your servants to speak your word with all
boldness, while you stretch out your hand to heal,
and signs and wonders are performed through
the name of your holy servant Jesus."

—ACTS 4:29–30

When she was around two, my daughter came home from preschool with a coloring page. On it, the teacher had written, "Katie needs to learn to color in the lines." I didn't worry about it. She was two, for heaven's sake.

A few days later, another paper came home, bearing a wildly colored cat. More emphatic this time, the teacher had requested, "Please work with Katie on coloring in the lines!"

I still couldn't rouse myself to care. Sorry. Developmental issues aside, learning conformity as the highest value has its pitfalls. It leaves you totally unprepared for the moments that God might call you to do something new.

Jesus, fill me with your spirit, so that I might not be constrained by convention as I live as your disciple.

September 17

When the young man heard this word, he went
away grieving, for he had many possessions.

—MATTHEW 19:22

We know the conversation. The young man had
asked what he should do to gain eternal life,
besides observing the commandments. "Sell what you
have and give to the poor, then follow me," is Jesus'
answer.

What held the young man back? What holds me
back?

And what do I feel as I walk away, acknowledging
my unwillingness? Am I sad? Or am I, honestly, just a
little bit relieved?

Jesus, speak to me about what I lack.

September 18

The sins of some people are conspicuous
and precede them to judgment, while the
sins of others follow them there.
—1 TIMOTHY 5:24

Every few years, television news rediscovers exorcisms. Accompanied by great publicity, footage is broadcast in which some poor, tormented soul is prayed over. Lots of people watch, some out of curiosity and some hoping to catch a glimpse of evil. It's all very exciting.

But usually, evil is not so exciting. It is subtle and hidden, even from the one in whose heart it seeks to burrow. Some evil can catch our attention, while some very successfully avoids it.

Lord, help me discern any darkness in my life, so that your light might dispel it.

September 19

Then one said, "I will surely return to you in
due season, and your wife Sarah shall have a son."
And Sarah was listening at the tent entrance
behind him. Now Abraham and Sarah were old,
advanced in age; it had ceased to be with Sarah
after the manner of women. So Sarah laughed to
herself, saying, "After I have grown old, and my
husband is old, shall I have pleasure?"

—GENESIS 18:10–12

I read all kinds of amazing things in Scripture:
that I am loved by God, that God's mercy knows
no bounds, that true happiness is found in simply
trusting in God.

It's amazing. Almost unbelievable. And at
times—bad times—it can almost seem like a joke.

Well, it's not.

*Heavenly Father, deepen my trust in your word,
no matter how strange it might seem.*

September 20

It is that very Spirit bearing witness with our
spirit that we are children of God, and if
children, then heirs, heirs of God and joint heirs
with Christ—if, in fact, we suffer with him so
that we may also be glorified with him.

—ROMANS 8:16–17

Once when my daughter was small, she stood in
front of me and ticked off, on her little fingers,
her future plans. "I gonna be a cheerleader, a fire-
fighter, and a ballerina."

She looked up at me. "What you gonna be when
you grow up?"

Good question. Some of us never stop asking that.
Which is okay, I think, as long as we never forget that
at the end of the day, no matter what, the only identity
that matters is that of being God's own child.

*Lord, in my uncertainty about life, I hold fast to you,
as your own.*

September 21

St. Matthew

As Jesus was walking along, he saw a man
called Matthew sitting at the tax booth;
and he said to him, "Follow me." And he
got up and followed him.

—MATTHEW 9:9

Matthew was a tax collector. Not a popular profession; as a matter of fact, it was one that placed
him outside the community of faith.

But Jesus called, nonetheless.

Sometimes we feel as if there are things about us
that place us beyond the reach of God's love, mercy, or
even interest. Not so.

"Follow me."

Jesus, open my ears to your voice calling me.
Help me set aside my feelings of unworthiness.

September 22

When I was a child, I spoke like a child, I thought
like a child, I reasoned like a child; when I
became an adult, I put an end to childish ways.

—1 CORINTHIANS 13:11

I flew in an airplane for the first time when I
was around seven years old. What I remember
most vividly was the shock and dismay I felt upon
discovering that clouds were not, as I had thought,
fluffy balls of cotton in the sky but simply mist.

So, decades ago, I reluctantly let go of my fantasy
about teddy bears dancing on clouds. But might there
be something else I'm holding onto? Am I still afraid
to confront the reality behind the fantasy?

*God of truth, here's an area of my life in which I still
cling to a myth. Give me the courage to walk through
it to the truth.*

September 23

Let anyone with ears listen!

—MATTHEW 11:15

Apleasant voice greeted me when I answered the telephone. She acted as if she knew me, but I had to ask, "Who is this?"

Well, it was my college friend Lucy, whose voice I had not heard in years. Of course I didn't recognize her, obscured as her tones were by years of intervening voices and the fading of memory.

We sometimes complain that it's hard to figure out if and when God is speaking to us. Perhaps we've just been out of touch.

Lord, I know you speak to me always. Help me clear time in my day to be present to you, so that I might come to recognize your voice.

September 24

If you want the picture of absolute trust, here it is: a five-month-old baby, picked up and whirled around in the air, gurgling with laughter, totally unafraid. It seems like nothing, but imagine how you'd feel if someone ten times your size suddenly picked you up and started spinning you that far above the ground.

What happens to that trust?

Well, it gets betrayed, doesn't it? It's one of the hardest things to do—to learn to trust again after we've been hurt.

Lord, there are reasons I find it difficult to trust sometimes. Here they are. Help me find a way through this hurt.

September 25

Of course, there is great gain in godliness combined with contentment; for we brought nothing into the world, so that we can take nothing out of it; but if we have food and clothing, we will be content with these.

—1 TIMOTHY 6:6–8

There is wisdom to be found in religions other than Christianity, and probably that which I've found to be most true is one of the Four Noble Truths of Buddhism: "All suffering is rooted in desire."

Although Christianity would caution that desire can be good—the desire for God, for example—it makes sense that desire can be negative, too. Even on the terrifically mundane level, say, of finding a Wednesday at work difficult to endure just because you can't stop wishing it was Friday.

Our own faith, rooted in Jesus, reminds us of the same truth many times. What peace or joy does desiring something or being anxious bring us? Why waste our time?

Jesus, may my greatest desire be to do your will.

September 26

Then the LORD called, "Samuel! Samuel!"
and he said, "Here I am!"
—1 SAMUEL 3:4

When I was about nineteen, for a while I thought that I might want to be a religious sister. I visited a convent, got to know a few sisters, and did some praying and thinking. I felt a pull to work in the church, and that seemed the most logical choice at the time.

So here I am, a couple of decades and five children later. Not in a convent.

Samuel had a few false starts as he tried to answer God's call that night. But eventually, he understood where God was—and where God wanted him to be.

Lord, you are still calling me. Am I where you want me to be?

September 27

Those who are unspiritual do not receive the gifts
of God's Spirit, for they are foolishness to them,
and they are unable to understand them because
they are spiritually discerned.

—1 CORINTHIANS 2:14

My teenaged son sat in the car after school,
staring out the window, not his usual chatty
self. My imagination raced. Something was obviously
wrong. How could I get it out of him? How could I
help? Would he open up to me? Poor kid. So, gingerly,
I asked him, "Is anything wrong?"

He looked at me. "Mom, did you know that Fred
McGriff hit thirty home runs every season for the past
six years? And only eleven other players have ever
done that?"

No, I didn't know that—and a few other things as
well, apparently.

*God of wisdom, help me to listen to those around me
and not assume that I know everything.*

September 28

For I am about to create new heavens
and a new earth;
the former things shall not be remembered
or come to mind.

—ISAIAH 65:17

Eighth grade was truly awful. I was a new kid in a new school in a new town, and a group of girls decided to pick on me, mostly because of the way I dressed, which was something I had no control over because my mother was, let us say, rather old fashioned.

So, yes, it was thirty years ago, but the embarrassment is not totally gone. I can still feel it, just a little, in certain situations. And it's not a particularly helpful feeling.

Maybe it's time to let go and let God do something new with that part of my life, to help me use it, perhaps, to grow in deeper understanding of others' pain, rather than just dwelling on my own.

Lord, renew my heart, and let me put the hurts of the past behind me.

September 29

STS. MICHAEL, GABRIEL, AND RAPHAEL

Bless the LORD, O you his angels,
you mighty ones who do his bidding,
obedient to his spoken word.
Bless the LORD, all his hosts,
his ministers that do his will.

—PSALM 103:20-21

When I think of angels, I think of a universe alive with God's power, teeming with energy and love. Good news in the air, all the time.

We wonder why we can't sense this presence these days. Perhaps it's because the air around us is filled with so much else. Who can hear anything in this din?

God of the universe, with your angels, I give you praise.

September 30

So then, each of us will be accountable to God.
—ROMANS 14:12

I can't even count the number of times it's happened. There I am, back up against the wall, deadline looming—at one time it was papers to grade, now it's articles or chapters to write—and somehow these pesky kids won't stop making demands.

I think, if only . . . if only I didn't have all this domestic stuff to do. If only the kids would stop bothering me, I could be so much further along, and I wouldn't be under this stress. I conveniently forget the time I wasted on the Internet last night or the few minutes, here and there, I spent flipping through channels or staring into space.

In matters great or small, the responsibility for my life is ultimately mine.

Loving Father, you place no obstacles in the way of my faith journey. Help me take responsibility for the times I stray.

October

October 1

ST. THÉRÈSE OF LISIEUX

At that time Jesus said, "I thank you, Father,
Lord of heaven and earth, because you have
hidden these things from the wise and the
intelligent and have revealed them to infants."

—MATTHEW 11:25

It's amazing that when she died of tuberculosis at
the age of twenty-four, St. Thérèse was known by
relatively few people. But a little more than a century
later, her witness and spirituality have influenced
millions, while most of the "celebrities" of her day
have sunk into obscurity.

So many of us are caught up in a culture of
achievement and fame. We think that the value of our
lives is determined by who knows about us and what
we accomplish in the world. Thérèse lived and wrote
of something completely different, a "little way" in
which we simply live in gratitude for the life God has
given us, serving and loving in any way we can.

No matter how small it seems.

*Jesus, teach me to follow you in humility, filling
every task with love.*

October 2

May our sons in their youth
be like plants full grown,
our daughters like corner pillars,
cut for the building of a palace.

—PSALM 144:12

The most wonderful thing about having children isn't in what they do for you, how cute they are, or how happy they make you. It's that really astonishing, awe-inspiring fact that somehow, in cooperating with God, you've set another human being on a journey in the world—a person who will influence the world, be influenced by it, have a unique relationship with God, and who will probably, in turn, make even more of God's children.

To be able to have done that is worth any price, I think.

Lord, I thank you for the gift of life.

October 3

"Do not judge, and you will not be judged; do
not condemn, and you will not be condemned.
Forgive, and you will be forgiven."

—LUKE 6:37

This isn't about ignoring sin. Quite the opposite,
for the entire passage ends with Jesus telling us to
be sure to tend to the beam of wood in our own eyes
so that we can see more clearly to remove the splinter
in another's.

Hmm.

I think it's really about humility. I sin; you sin.
You sometimes need help to see clearly, and so
do I. Our reference point isn't our own supposed
superiority. Our reference point is God, as we journey
to him together.

Jesus, what blinds me? Give me humility.

October 4

May I never boast of anything except the cross
of our Lord Jesus Christ, by which the world
has been crucified to me, and I to the world.
—GALATIANS 6:14

There are images of St. Francis that are pleasantly inspiring, and those are the images we tend to dwell on: lover of creation, the freedom of detachment from the world, brother in community.

Not so pleasant are the other realities: the poverty, his presence to the diseased and rejected, the physical deterioration, the pain.

St. Francis bears all this, too. Because St. Francis bears Christ.

Lord Jesus, guide my steps as I seek to journey with you as St. Francis did.

October 5

Hear my voice, O God, in my complaint;
preserve my life from the dread enemy.
—Psalm 64:1

My daughter and I were walking to the library on a path that took us by a small lake populated with waterfowl. A large, white goose stood looking at us from across the road. Without warning, he decided we were trouble and lunged toward us in a rage.

Another time, down by another lake, my son lifted a board he was going to use to untangle his fishing line, which was trapped in the weeds at some distance from shore. He didn't see the snake, but I did, as it erupted from its rest under the board.

Hidden deep within me are dangerous urges, inclinations, and temptations. I pray God protect us from all the dangers that await.

Lord, you are my refuge. Give me eyes to see and strength to pursue holiness.

October 6

A poor widow came and put in two small copper coins, which are worth a penny. Then he called his disciples and said to them, "Truly I tell you, this poor widow has put in more than all those who are contributing to the treasury. For all of them have contributed out of their abundance; but she out of her poverty has put in everything she had, all she had to live on."

—MARK 12:42–44

Tempted to congratulate myself on my faith, I may consider the poor widow.
Where's my sacrifice?
Honestly, now. Where?

Jesus, be with me as I consider what I've been given—and what I can give.

I have swept away your transgressions like a cloud,
and your sins like mist;
return to me, for I have redeemed you.

—ISAIAH 44:22

Ihad borne a sin on my conscience for a while. I finally went to a shrine where I could sit with a priest I didn't know and lay it all out.

"I absolve you," he said.

And I walked away, wondering. Surely not. It's not that it was easy—I had borne consequences of this sin, and they had hurt. I had a penance. No, it's that something in me couldn't believe the reality behind the words *mercy* and *forgiveness*.

But it's true. It's also true that there's only one force in the universe that would like me to give in and refuse to accept that mercy—and it's not God.

Merciful God, help me accept your forgiveness.

"Then the manager said to himself, 'What will I do, now that my master is taking the position away from me? I am not strong enough to dig, and I am ashamed to beg. I have decided what to do so that, when I am dismissed as manager, people may welcome me into their homes.'"

—LUKE 16:3–4

Jesus tells the parable of a man who has been fired as manager of an estate. In the face of this disaster, the manager doesn't despair; he gets to work. He goes out to those indebted to his master and promptly reduces their debts, giving rise to much goodwill and assuring that he will have friends once he is displaced.

All of us face disaster and change in our lives. Some of those experiences are our own fault; others just happen to us. We may respond in any number of ways. We may feel sorry for ourselves, or we may rage against those who have done this to us.

Or we may be like the wily manager by trying to bring some good out of the situation and move on. What good reason is there not to?

Heavenly Father, help me discern the good that you want to bring out of hardship.

October 9

But the LORD said to Samuel, "Do not look on his appearance or on the height of his stature, because I have rejected him; for the LORD does not see as mortals see; they look on the outward appearance, but the LORD looks on the heart."

—1 SAMUEL 16:7

My high-school religion teacher was a young religious sister whom we all adored. One day she was speaking to us about the habit, which she wore, and not unwillingly.

She told us, however, about a woman she visited every Saturday morning. She brought the elderly woman groceries, helped her around the house, and visited with her. The woman was blind.

"I really don't think she cares what I wear," mused Sister. "I hope she can tell I love Jesus by how I treat her."

Lord, take away my concerns about appearance, and mold my heart.

October 10

Put away from you all bitterness and wrath
and anger and wrangling and slander, together
with all malice, and be kind to one another,
tenderhearted, forgiving one another, as God
in Christ has forgiven you.

—EPHESIANS 4:31–32

I saw an old friend from college the other day, for the first time in twenty years. There was something really fundamental about his present life that he didn't share. I know about it from someone else he's told, and I gave him a couple of friendly openings to share. But he didn't.

I didn't push him, because it's none of my business, but my ego was a little bruised. More important, I guess, it moved me to think about how I present myself. Do I let the compassion I honestly feel reveal itself? Or do people see something else?

Lord Jesus, let your compassionate love shine through me.

October 11

They devoted themselves to the apostles'
teaching and fellowship, to the breaking
of bread and the prayers.

—ACTS 2:42

My high-school religion students were fond of declaring that they were really beyond the "obligation" to attend Mass. After all, given the freedom, they would certainly set aside plenty of time during the week to pray and worship in their own way—or maybe not, they would finally admit, when pressed to be honest.

My own will isn't infallible or always trustworthy. Even now, the sense of an obligation can be useful, as it pushes me into the space where I can hear God more clearly than if left purely to my own, undependable devices.

Lord, teach me to be faithful in my prayer and receptive toward what you would say to me.

October 12

When they asked him to stay longer, he declined; but on taking leave of them, he said, "I will return to you, if God wills." Then he set sail from Ephesus.

—ACTS 18:20–21

Within the span of a few months, I observed two grieving families. In one, the young father had passed away after a protracted battle with leukemia. Finally, there was nothing to be done, and, surrounded by family and friends singing hymns and praying with him at home, he passed to God.

In the other, a middle-aged mother discovered she had cancer, and, without telling anyone in her family of the diagnosis, she got up early, went into the bathroom, and shot herself.

Hard and tragic. But a strong lesson in the fruit of cooperating with God's will, as mysterious and painful as it might be.

Lord, strengthen me in my journey.

October 13

Keep alert, stand firm in your faith,
be courageous, be strong.
—1 CORINTHIANS 16:13

Standing firm isn't as easy as it sounds. All kinds of factors can come into play. Even physical ones.

One of the great struggles of my life has been to figure out how the emotional changes of my monthly hormonal variations affect the rest of my life. It is a great mystery to me; I like to think of myself as a free agent, but sometimes, fighting the predictable depression at one point in the month and embracing the feeling of great creativity at another, I have to wonder.

I don't understand it. But there it is, and I must trust that it's given by God for a reason.

Creator God, help me accept myself and work through and with the realities of my physical life, staying strong in you.

October 14

Train yourself in godliness, for, while physical
training is of some value, godliness is valuable
in every way, holding promise for both the
present life and the life to come.

—1 TIMOTHY 4:7–8

Well. How much time have I spent tending to
my physical self this week—considering my
diet, making sure I work out, discussing diet plans
with friends—and how much time have I devoted to
strengthening and toning my spiritual life?

Lord, fix my sights on the health of my soul.

October 15

St. Teresa of Ávila

"If you belonged to the world, the world would love you as its own. Because you do not belong to the world, but I have chosen you out of the world— therefore the world hates you."

—John 15:19

✤

There is much to love about St. Teresa of Ávila: her brilliance, spiritual wisdom, will, energy, and unfettered passion for God.

But it's helpful to note, too, that Teresa took a while to grow and bear fruit. In fact, for the first part of her adult life, she lived in a convent, yes, but the life of a typical wealthy nun of her time: comfortable, sociable, and not terribly concerned with the cross.

But things changed for Teresa when, around the age of forty, she was drawn into greater intimacy with God. The old ways had to be left behind, and in joy, she took off her shoes (literally) and set off to follow Jesus.

It's never too late. The rut is never so deep that we can't climb out.

✤

Heavenly Father, give me the courage to travel new paths with you.

October 16

Now may our Lord Jesus Christ himself and
God our Father, who loved us and through
grace gave us eternal comfort and good hope,
comfort your hearts and strengthen them in
every good work and word.

—2 Thessalonians 2:16–17

I once had a very difficult decision to make. There
was no way, I thought, that I could make what I
knew was the right one. But then I had reason to take
an unexpectedly lengthy bus trip.

During that trip, I had time to consider what it
meant to be a disciple. Did it mean I'll follow, but not
now? Is that what Jesus did? Or did it mean something
else? If I couldn't follow Jesus now, what was the point
of even pretending I was a disciple? Isn't this what it's
all about?

And miraculously (I mean it), by the end of the
bus trip, I found the strength to do what I had to do.
With even a little joy.

Jesus, I ponder hard choices I must make.
Hold me up.

October 17

Now Rachel had taken the household gods and put
them in the camel's saddle, and sat on them. Laban
felt all about in the tent, but did not find them.

— Genesis 31:34

Rachel was clearly not completely with the "one
true God" program yet. In fleeing from her angry
father, along with her husband, Jacob, and her sister
(and Jacob's other wife), Leah, she found that she
couldn't leave her idols behind.

I wonder if I'm with the program myself. I say the
creed at Mass and claim that God is first. But is this
the way I live?

Or am I hiding a few idols—the esteem of others,
my appearance, money—just to be safe?

*Lord, you are my God, the source of meaning and
happiness in my life.*

October 18

Then Jesus said to him, "Today salvation has come
to this house, because he too is a son of Abraham."
—LUKE 19:9

I occasionally visit monasteries and contemplate
the gift of that kind of life. Oh, monks are
still human, and their communities bear all the
dynamics of human communities. But sometimes
I think, wouldn't it be nice? Wouldn't it be easier to
nurture intimacy with God without all of these . . .
distractions?

That's one way to look at it. Probably the wrong
way. Monastic or domestic, saint or sinner—wherever
and whoever we are, Jesus comes to all our houses.

Jesus, I welcome you into my life as it is.

October 19

STS. ISAAC JOGUES AND JEAN DE BRÉBEUF, AND COMPANIONS

"I give you a new commandment, that you
love one another. Just as I have loved you,
you also should love one another."

—JOHN 13:34

The saints we honor today all came to the shores of this continent, moved by love. The story of Isaac Jogues—who was captured, escaped, and then willingly returned to minister in danger once again—is familiar. But that of Jean de Brébeuf is perhaps not.

Jean de Brébeuf ministered in much the same way as his fellows, but he left something rather interesting behind. It was a guide, of sorts, written for those who would seek to minister among the native peoples. The most important point, he said, was this: "You must love these Hurons, ransomed by the blood of the Son of God, as brothers."

Not pity or control. Love as your brothers, for that is who they are.

Loving God, teach me to love all people as your saints have loved them.

October 20

Again I saw that under the sun the race is not to
the swift, nor the battle to the strong, nor bread
to the wise, nor riches to the intelligent, nor favor
to the skillful; but time and chance happen
to them all.

—ECCLESIASTES 9:11

If I had left the house five minutes earlier, if I hadn't misplaced my keys and had to search for them, I'd have been involved in that accident I just passed. I came this close to attending a different college than I did. If I had, I never would have met the people I did, and my life might have been completely different. Even the children I have would not exist, just as I wouldn't exist if my own parents had made different choices.

Sometimes I'm overwhelmed by the roles that chance and contingency play in life. It is all such a tremendous mystery to me—how God's ways, our ways, and what seems like chance all intersect to make life as it is. To think that I can make plans—what folly!

Not that I don't keep trying.

*Lord, guide me through the mystery of life, to do
your will.*

October 21

I will satisfy the weary,
and all who are faint I will replenish.
—JEREMIAH 31:25

When I was working outside the home as a teacher, I was exhausted most of the time. Now I work in the home, as a writer and mother of a toddler (not to speak of several other older kids), and while I'm not exhausted, I'm tired in different ways.

For example, to be really honest, sometimes I just get tired of parenting. I've been doing it for twenty-two years, and there are days when I would just like all the children to learn to fend for themselves, even if they're only three years old. It's a tough world, kid.

But around the corner, as close as God's untiring love for me, there is rest.

Lord, here's what makes me so tired. Refresh and strengthen me.

October 22

Then I saw a new heaven and a new earth.
—REVELATION 21:1

One morning, as we left for church, we observed a rabbit lying motionless in our backyard. We thought it was strange but also thought that if it was hurt, we'd tend to it when we returned.

Too late. When we returned, a hawk was busy with his breakfast. In fact, he had probably started the whole business, capturing and then dropping the poor rabbit from a height to injure and immobilize it. I wrote a column about this and received many outraged letters in response. Why hadn't we rescued the bunny? How cold!

I was puzzled. It was sad, but it was also life. Hawks don't live on salad. One rabbit rescued, one squirrel on the run.

Lord God, help me accept the mysteries of creation, even the painful ones, knowing that in your new creation, death will be no more.

October 23

It is actually reported that there is sexual
immorality among you, and of a kind
that is not found even among pagans; for
a man is living with his father's wife.
And you are arrogant!

—1 CORINTHIANS 5:1–2

When I was in college, I was part of a religious campus ministry group. We were active and enthusiastic, we attended daily Mass, we planned liturgies and retreats.

And some of us also did some crazy, bad stuff. As I recall, we came to believe that our behavior was excused, in a way, by our intense religious involvement. We felt really good about life, and we associated it with God. So we assumed that everything we did was somehow justified and okay.

Well, it wasn't, and this was a useful, if long and painful, lesson for me. Do I sometimes labor under the assumption that because I'm confident in God's love, everything is permissible?

*Lord, guide me as I examine my life and my heart.
Forgive me for taking your love for granted.*

October 24

You open your hand,
satisfying the desire of every living thing.
The LORD is just in all his ways,
and kind in all his doings.
The LORD is near to all who call on him,
to all who call on him in truth.
—PSALM 145:16–18

My roommate at the writers' conference was a Spanish poet and artist who daunted and fascinated me with her sophistication, her verve, and her bluntness. I don't think I told her much about myself, but I must have said enough for her to notice a certain lack of confidence, perhaps even a rather defeatist attitude toward life.

One night, I was walking back to my room from an author reading, through a misty rain. Maria suddenly appeared in the middle of the sidewalk, like a vision. She shook her finger at me. "You deserve," she said strongly. "You deserve!"

And she kept walking, disappearing in the mountain fog.

Lord, you desire my peace and happiness. Show me where to find it and how to treasure it.

$$\mathscr{October\ 25}$$

Do not be conformed to this world, but be
transformed by the renewing of your minds, so
that you may discern what is the will of God—
what is good and acceptable and perfect.

—ROMANS 12:2

All morning long, I'd been thinking about the talk
I was scheduled to give. Then, as I was walking
out the door, the telephone rang. It was one of my
sons, upset over difficult news that put everything I'd
been dwelling on in a completely new light.

It wasn't good news, and, in relation to it, my
concerns of the morning seemed pathetically trivial.
I didn't want to go to my speaking engagement, but
I really had no choice. So I went, but in a completely
changed frame of mind—for the better, I hope. Maybe
that change in outlook made my words more useful to
my audience.

Conversion is rather like that. Life goes on, but it
looks completely different in the light of the news of
God's love and redemption.

*Lord Jesus, help me let go of my own priorities and
allow your will to rule my life.*

October 26

Set a guard over my mouth, O LORD;
keep watch over the door of my lips.

—PSALM 141:3

Many years ago, I suffered a miscarriage. An acquaintance was offering me sympathy. She actually said to me, "It's too bad, but I guess it's better than getting a broken doll, isn't it?"

Lord, forgive me for the times I have hurt others with my words, even unintentionally.

October 27

For to this you have been called, because Christ
also suffered for you, leaving you an example,
so that you should follow in his steps.

—1 PETER 2:21

We modern folk often think that the way to deal
with suffering is simply to avoid it.

But I have to think, honestly, have I ever learned
anything important except through suffering?

*Jesus, today I follow your way, through suffering
and joy.*

October 28

Is not my house like this with God?
For he has made with me an everlasting covenant,
ordered in all things and secure.
Will he not cause to prosper
all my help and my desire?

—2 Samuel 23:5

On a visit to New York City years ago, we made the brilliant decision of driving into Manhattan at around four in the afternoon. We had time to kill, so why not?

Of course, we eventually discovered why not, as we crept in horrendous traffic for what seemed like days. Our two-year-old, tired and frustrated, started whining, "I want somepin'." He wanted to get out, he wanted food, he just wanted the present situation to end. He kept it up for a very long time, all the way back to Connecticut.

We can feel like that, too—dissatisfied, restless, just wanting a change, no matter how undefined. Perhaps all that "somepin'" could be discovered, if I just turned my heart to God.

Lord, I lay out my desires before you. Help me see beyond them to all that you give.

October 29

He said to them, "But who do you say that I am?"
Simon Peter answered, "You are the Messiah,
the Son of the living God."
—MATTHEW 16:15–16

There are lots of places I could look to learn about Jesus, to satisfy my curiosity and answer my questions. Movies tell his story. Television documentaries and even popular novels purport to reveal deep secrets or new understandings of Jesus. It's all very exciting.

Or . . . I could simply crack open a Gospel. And listen.

Lord Jesus, I want to know you more deeply.

October 30

Let us run with perseverance the race that is set
before us, looking to Jesus the pioneer and perfecter
of our faith, who for the sake of the joy that was
set before him endured the cross, disregarding its
shame, and has taken his seat at the right hand of
the throne of God.

—HEBREWS 12:1–2

I sometimes watch sports events and wonder, why don't they just play one quarter? Why don't they just drive one lap? Why not just one hole? Or one inning? It often just comes down to that, anyway.

Well, that's because there is something to be learned along the way, in those other quarters, laps, and innings. How you play, what happens to you, how you persevere—all of it works together in the end.

I suppose it is the same with our journey to God. Why these many (for most of us) years of life, with all their mysteries, ups, and downs? There is something about how you make the journey, and not just the bare fact that you arrive.

Loving God, thank you for the ways in which this race I run enriches, teaches, and strengthens me.

October 31

I commune with my heart in the night;
I meditate and search my spirit.

—Psalm 77:6

Whether we believe in ghosts, most of us would agree that we've been haunted at one time or another. Haunted by past mistakes, by loss, by people we've hurt, and by missed opportunities.

The past can have a great deal of power as it haunts us.

Why do we let it?

Lord, help me let go of the past and embrace the present.

November

November 1

ALL SAINTS' DAY

"These are they who have come out of the great
ordeal; they have washed their robes and made
them white in the blood of the Lamb."
—REVELATION 7:14

Growing up, I never heard much about saints,
much less their earthly remains. Stories about
saints just didn't factor into my catechesis, and the
churches I attended were relatively unadorned, with
hardly a saint's image in sight.

So imagine my surprise when, well into my thirties, I walked into an old church in Milwaukee and
beheld a solid wall full of saints' relics on display in
their small gold and glass reliquaries.

It wasn't just surprise I felt, though. It was relief.

Relief that in this journey of faith, I wasn't alone,
and here was the proof. The relics that surrounded
me were visible signs of the invisible communion of
saints, brothers and sisters who had loved God, lived
for him, and were there to support me—and you—as
we travel the same, joyful path.

Lord, thank you for the friendship of the saints.

November 2

ALL SOULS' DAY

But he said to them, "Do not be alarmed; you are
looking for Jesus of Nazareth, who was crucified.
He has been raised; he is not here."

—MARK 16:6

Today we remember, mourn, and pray for the
faithful departed. We're not the first to do this. A
couple of thousand years ago, some women watched
their friend and teacher die. They saw his lifeless
body carried to a tomb and saw the tomb sealed with
a stone, separating them from their loved one forever.

Or so they thought, until three days later when
they found the tomb empty and heard these words:
"Do not be alarmed." The words came first from the
angel, and then from the teacher himself—Jesus, no
longer dead but alive. No longer gone but present. The
call was clear: Be not afraid, for death has been con-
quered and is no longer the end.

So today we remember, we mourn—because we
are human—and we pray. But we do so in hope, no
longer afraid.

Loving God, may the souls of the faithful departed
rest in peace.

November 3

"But when you give a banquet, invite the poor, the crippled, the lame, and the blind. And you will be blessed, because they cannot repay you, for you will be repaid at the resurrection of the righteous."

—LUKE 14:13–14

There are days when so much of what we do seems to just sink down a black hole, doesn't it?

The work we do at home or on the job seems unappreciated. Our family members are quick to notice what we neglected but seem indifferent to what we did manage to accomplish.

Jesus warns us against doing good with the hope of being repaid. It's natural to wish for appreciation or recompense for the good we do. But when Jesus tells his dinner host to invite guests who cannot possibly ever repay him, he's telling all of us that the best reason to do good is, simply, to do good.

Jesus, let all my actions come out of the desire to love.

"At the time for the dinner he sent his slave to
say to those who had been invited, 'Come;
for everything is ready now.' But they all alike
began to make excuses. The first said to him,
'I have bought a piece of land, and I must go out
and see it; please accept my regrets.'"

—LUKE 14:17–18

How do we excuse ourselves from following
the Lord? For me, it usually takes the form of
procrastination. *Not now,* I think. *I can't quite cope
with that part of Jesus' teaching now. Later I'll probably
be able to. But not now.*

And why don't I want to accept Jesus' invitation
at that moment? Usually it's because it would require
sacrifice. Sacrifice of pride, money, time, or, most
important, my own precious worldview.

Your excuses might not be the same as mine. After
all, in the parable Jesus tells, there's no lack of variety
in the reasons people decline their invitations.

But no matter what the reason, the outcome is
the same: in believing that we know better, we miss
the party.

*Lord, I pray for the grace to accept your invitation
to love.*

November 5

"Are not five sparrows sold for two pennies? Yet not one of them is forgotten in God's sight. But even the hairs of your head are all counted. Do not be afraid; you are of more value than many sparrows."

—LUKE 12:6–7

It's ironically striking how closed we modern folks really are. You wouldn't know it, since we seem so very much into sharing our stories and feelings, we're so interested in intimate gossip, and we're so darned immodest overall.

However, being truly and intimately known remains, as it always has been, a terrifying prospect. We all say that being known, understood, and accepted is exactly what we want. But if that's true, why do we put up such a fight when we get close to intimacy?

Even our spiritual lives are affected by our fear of being known. Jesus tells us not to worry—that God knows us deeply—but sometimes those words can sound more like a threat than a promise. Our guilt, our poor sense of self, not to speak of our pride, all conspire to shield us from God's loving, knowing gaze.

Lord, today I open my life to you, holding nothing back.

November 6

Sing to him, sing praises to him;
tell of all his wonderful works.
—PSALM 105:2

My oldest son calls me regularly and predictably from his college dorm around midterms and finals. Every time, the problem is the same, and it breaks my maternal heart: He feels overwhelmed, overworked, and despondent about his prospects. And every time, my attempts at comfort translate into the same words of advice. Take one task at a time. Don't worry about the things you can't control, only those matters that you can. And give thanks.

It's an interesting exercise. Each time you're tempted to wish that life was other than it is, give thanks. Each time you're tempted to fall into despair, sing God's praise. Each time you're wondering if this is really all there is, sing of God's wondrous deeds, for they are great, and our troubles really are comparatively small.

Lord, today I sing your praise. I give thanks for the gift of life.

"Keep awake therefore, for you know
neither the day nor the hour."
—MATTHEW 25:13

My friend told me about her bone cancer on Halloween night. She sat on her daughter's front porch. Children's laughter drifted up and down the street in the cool darkness. "On the bone scan," she said, "my shoulder blades are black with cancer."

For days afterward, between my prayers, all I could think about was what it could possibly be like— to walk through your day knowing that an enemy was working hard within your body, and that it could win, very possibly in only a matter of months.

But then, just as quickly, another thought followed. Isn't that the way it is for all of us, anyway?

I say this not to be morbid but simply to be real, as real as the warning offered in the Gospels. We just don't know when the time will come. Are we ready?

Lord, help me embrace the meaning of my journey here on earth, and ready me for eternal life with you.

November 8

"Which one of you, having a hundred sheep and losing one of them, does not leave the ninety-nine in the wilderness and go after the one that is lost until he finds it? When he has found it, he lays it on his shoulders and rejoices."

—LUKE 15:4–5

Perhaps you remember the feeling of being lost. I sure do. I was around six, with my parents in a department store. I turned to say something to the person next to me, thinking it was my dad. It wasn't.

The details of the event fade, but the feelings don't at all: the hard rock that used to be my stomach, the trembling, and, finally, the total, blessed wave of relief when I was found.

In the darkness of life, we can still feel lost in many ways. Why am I here? Have my failings put me outside God's embrace? Jesus' words reassure us that he is always looking for us.

Loving Father, thank you for embracing me when I feel lost.

November 9

DEDICATION OF ST. JOHN LATERAN

Come to him, a living stone, though rejected by
mortals yet chosen and precious in God's sight,
and like living stones, let yourselves be built
into a spiritual house, to be a holy priesthood,
to offer spiritual sacrifices acceptable to God
through Jesus Christ.

—1 PETER 2:4–5

Today we celebrate the Dedication of the Lateran
Basilica in Rome, the pope's home church.

I've had many "home churches" in my life. I've
belonged to very with-it university parishes and barely
with-it rural Catholic missions. My home parishes have
had cool Mexican tiles, life-size crucifixes, lots of art,
and no art. The music in my home churches has been
contemporary, traditional, wonderful, and dreadful.

But every home parish shares something: Jesus.
So when we celebrate this beautiful, historic Roman
church built centuries ago, we're really celebrating the
Jesus who dwells there, in the pope's church, and in
the living stones of our own communities.

Father, thank you for the gift of my parish.

November 10

To all God's beloved in Rome,
who are called to be saints:
Grace to you and peace from God our Father
and the Lord Jesus Christ.
—ROMANS 1:7

These first few verses of Paul's letter to the Romans overflow with "call's." Paul is called, the gentiles are called, and Paul's readers are called. Everyone, it seems, is called, to be a saint, no less. But what about our more specific callings?

We grudgingly suspect that it would be easier to figure out our callings if we had it as simple as the likes of Moses, the apostles, and, yes, Paul himself. Nice, clear, dramatic calls beckoning us from burning bushes, the lakeshore, and the clouds above. Most of our calls rarely rise above the level of "What's for dinner, Mom?"

So, we wait in vain for the dramatic, while everyday life swamps us with those ordinary calls. Might our answer be right in our midst, calling us to listen with St. Thérèse, who once wrote, "To ecstasy, I prefer the monotony of sacrifice"?

*Lord, give me the eyes to see and the ears to hear
your call in my everyday life.*

November 11

Until a spirit from on high is poured out on us,
and the wilderness becomes a fruitful field,
and the fruitful field is deemed a forest.
Then justice will dwell in the wilderness,
and righteousness abide in the fruitful field.

—ISAIAH 32:15–16

A few months ago, for the first time in my life, I saw a real desert. Brought to Phoenix for a speaking engagement, as I was driven around, I couldn't stop remarking to my undoubtedly bemused host, "It really is a desert!"

It was a strange sort of beautiful to my east-of-the-Mississippi eyes. Astonishing as well was the fact that human beings have brought life into this desert, flourishing against great odds.

God, in his power, can do the same—and more—in the dry, desert places of my spirit. Perhaps even in the places I have believed, for a long time, that nothing could ever grow.

God of Life, water and nourish my spirit so that every corner of it might flourish.

November 12

[F]or he makes his sun rise on the evil
and on the good, and sends rain on
the righteous and on the unrighteous.

—MATTHEW 5:45

God loves the most unpleasant person I know just as much as he loves me. The person who hurt me terribly God treasures as deeply as he treasures me.

No more, no less. Holiness is seeing and living in the midst of others, with the mind of Christ.

Lord, help me to see all people through your loving eyes.

ST. FRANCES XAVIER CABRINI

"The kingdom of God is not coming with things
that can be observed; nor will they say,
'Look, here it is!' or 'There it is!' For, in fact,
the kingdom of God is among you."

—LUKE 17:20–21

For some, Jesus' words about the kingdom might be an invitation to look inward. For others, including St. Frances Xavier Cabrini, it was the opposite.

If you want to get tired, read about St. Frances Xavier Cabrini's travels for the kingdom: from Italy to the United States, where she worked in New York, Chicago, Colorado, and many points in between and beyond. In all these places, she founded hospitals, schools, and orphanages—places where the neediest could be touched by God's love and healing.

God's kingdom is among us, and since we are all brothers and sisters living in the world God made, the possibilities of this kingdom are as near—or as far—as we choose to see.

Heavenly Father, help me discern the power and possibility of your kingdom among all people.

November 14

Jesus said to him, "What do you want me
to do for you?" The blind man said to him,
"My teacher, let me see again."

—MARK 10:51

We often get it in our heads that we know
exactly what other people need. Faced with a
crisis, we take control, dispense advice, and get busy
fixing things. How often do we stop and ask the one
we're helping, "Tell me what it is you need me to do
right now"?

This is exactly what Jesus says to a blind beggar
he encounters as he's leaving Jericho.

Perhaps we could take a hint from Jesus.
Confronted with frustrated spouses, confused kids,
or bereaved friends, we could put our own opinions
aside, humbly approach the ones we love, and simply
ask, "What do you want me to do for you?"

Spirit, give me wisdom as I seek to help those in need.

November 15

"Then the one who had received the one talent also
came forward, saying, 'Master, I knew that you
were a harsh man, reaping where you did not sow,
and gathering where you did not scatter seed;
so I was afraid, and I went and hid your talent in
the ground.'"

—MATTHEW 25:24–25

The parable is about a master who entrusts his
money to his servants while he goes on a journey.
Upon his return, most of the servants have made a
profit, but one has done nothing but bury his portion
in the ground. His excuse? Despite his master's
instructions, he was still paralyzed by fear. He decided
he knew better than his master.

How often do we respond to God in exactly the
same way? Jesus tells us to put God first and let material
needs take care of themselves. He tells us that God
wants to forgive us our sins. He lets us know that happiness
lies in the way of forgiveness and love.

Do our lives reflect trust in that Good News? Or
do they express our fears, not to speak of our unspoken
convictions that we know better than the master?

Jesus, I put my trust in the path you walk.

November 16

"Those who are considered worthy of a place in
that age and in the resurrection from the
dead neither marry nor are given in marriage.
Indeed they cannot die anymore, because
they are like angels and are children of God,
being children of the resurrection."

—LUKE 20:35–36

When I was a child, I imagined heaven as a place in which all my favorite fictional characters were alive. You can see what my priorities were.

For months, my daughter was bothered by the question of what age we would be in heaven, until she finally decided that it would be the age at which we had been happiest on earth.

Here, the Sadducees come to Jesus with curious, tricky questions about whom a woman who had been married seven times would be married to in heaven.

Our curiosity is natural, but it should never distract us from the truth that we know for sure: In heaven, we will find our fulfillment and our joy simply because we will be with God.

Lord, may every moment of my life on earth prepare me for life with you—the joy of heaven, a joy beyond my imagining.

November 17

Where can I go from your spirit?
Or where can I flee from your presence?
—PSALM 139:7

When I was a student, like most of my friends, I kept a countdown calendar. Beginning around February, when life was dreariest and summer seemed furthest away, I'd cross those days off, one by one. (Who am I kidding? I did the same thing when I was teaching!)

How much of life do we spend waiting for happiness, for what we think will be better times?

Do we see where that leads? Maybe just straight to the end of life, where we will look back and wonder why we couldn't just find peace where we were, rather than always saving it for later.

Lord, increase my capacity to take joy in your presence right now.

November 18

Do not lag in zeal, be ardent in spirit,
serve the Lord. Rejoice in hope, be
patient in suffering, persevere in prayer.

—ROMANS 12:11–12

It is easy, sometimes, to grow weary of prayer. Physical fatigue is not the problem. No, it's the temptation to let hope drain while we wait for answers.

When those answers don't seem to come, we can tire. We wonder if anyone is there. We wonder if we're just not worthy of God's attention.

Paul reminds us to persevere. And we remember the times that Jesus reminds us that, if human beings respond to requests from those they love, God surely will, too.

Father, as I lay my needs before you, help me trust that you are listening.

November 19

"Be dressed for action and have your lamps lit; be like those who are waiting for their master to return from the wedding banquet, so that they may open the door for him as soon as he comes and knocks."

—LUKE 12:35–36

My part of the country must have the most unpredictable weather in the land. More times than I can count, television weather reporters have filled the air with dire warnings of huge snowstorms, everyone rushing to the grocery store and emptying the shelves, only to be met with days of sunny skies.

It works the other way, too. One Christmas Eve, we went to bed, told to expect nothing but a chill. We awoke to a foot of snow. We didn't expect it and we weren't prepared.

We can be certain, though, that this moment Jesus describes will, indeed, occur. If not tonight, it still probably will be sooner than I think. Am I ready?

Lord, help me live a life of joyful expectation, awaiting fullness of life with you.

November 20

"Tell us, when will this be, and what will be the sign
that all these things are about to be accomplished?"
Then Jesus began to say to them, "Beware that no
one leads you astray. Many will come in my name
and say, 'I am he!' and they will lead many astray."

—MARK 13:4–6

Over time, parents become experts at interpreting
signs and foretelling the future. The briefest sigh
tells us how much of dinner will be willingly eaten and
how much will be fought over. Whispered telephone
conversations let us know, without doubt, that trouble
is in the offing.

But Jesus tells us to be a bit more careful in trying
to interpret signs of his coming. We are understand-
ably curious and anxious about these events, but the
mind of God is a lot harder to read than the mind of
an eleven-year-old, no matter what false prophets and
self-proclaimed end-times experts try to tell us. It is
best to wait in trust and simple hope, rather than in
anxious speculation.

*Spirit, help me discern truth from falsehood as
I joyfully await your coming.*

November 21

PRESENTATION OF MARY

Sing and rejoice, O daughter Zion! For lo, I will
come and dwell in your midst, says the Lord.
—ZECHARIAH 2:10

The Feast of the Presentation of the Blessed Virgin
Mary points to an important truth about Mary:
As Mary's parents presented her at the temple, they
offered thanks for their child. In dedicating her to
God, they expressed faith that her life was a blessing
given for a wonderful purpose.

It was true of Mary, and it is true for us. One of
the reasons Mary is so important is that, in her, we
can see all of God's promises fulfilled. God promises
redemption, wholeness, and eternal life. Mary is the
recipient of these gifts—and they are offered to us
as well.

Every day we have a chance to present ourselves
to God, give thanks, and express the faith that our
lives are gifts with wonderful purpose.

*Lord, I thank you for the gift of my life. I present it to
you, with the prayer that I may always use this gift
for your glory.*

November 22

Pilate asked him, "So you are a king?" Jesus
answered, "You say that I am a king. For this
I was born, and for this I came into the world,
to testify to the truth. Everyone who belongs
to the truth listens to my voice."

—JOHN 18:37

As the liturgical year draws to a close, we celebrate
Christ as our king. This may be hard for us to
understand, formed as we are by the idea of kingship
as a role of pomp and domination. The Gospel
definition of kingship is much different, though.
Imagine any other people remembering their king
by telling the story of the interrogation before his
seemingly ignoble death.

As Jesus stands before Pilate, we see clearly what
Jesus' lordship means in our world and in our lives.
It means, in a word, love. In his great love, our king
humbles himself. He offers his life in sacrifice and service. His kingdom, then, bears the same marks; in it,
forgiveness reigns and love rules.

And as the King lives, so do his joyful subjects.

Lord Jesus, today I accept gladly the reign of your love.

I commend to you our sister Phoebe, a deacon of
the church at Cenchreae, so that you may welcome
her in the Lord as is fitting for the saints, . . .
Greet Prisca and Aquila, who work with me in
Christ Jesus, and who risked their necks for my
life, to whom not only I give thanks, but also all
the churches of the Gentiles.

—ROMANS 16:1–4

Confronted with a list of people who may have been
Paul's friends but about whom I know nothing,
I'm tempted to just skip it and move on to something
more obviously spiritual.

But no, I'll stop. For when I take the time to read
slowly the names of Paul's friends and coworkers, and
when I reflect on the warmth and strength so obvious in this Christ-centered community, I'm moved to
make my own list of companions in the faith. They are
people I know personally, and some I don't, but they
are working together to proclaim the Good News, in
ways great and small.

*Loving God, thank you for the companions you have
given me on this journey. May I be encouraging and
helpful to them, as they are to me.*

November 24

Why do you pass judgment on your brother
or sister? Or you, why do you despise your
brother or sister? For we will all stand before
the judgment seat of God.

—ROMANS 14:10

He worked the night shift at the hospital. She
taught high school during the day. They saw each
other rarely, it seemed, but had been happily married
for twenty-five years.

Sniping from outsiders, though, was a constant.
"What kind of a marriage is that?" they'd ask. "They
must not really like each other."

It's tempting to judge other people's paths to
happiness. That's the kind of judgment I think Paul
is talking of here. Some early Christians integrated
Paul's insights about grace, freedom, and the law
into their lives; others maintained observance. Don't
concern yourselves, Paul says. Trust that whatever is
done, is done out of love for the Lord, and leave the
judgment up to him.

*Lord, make me attentive to your workings in my own
heart and accepting of the paths others choose.*

November 25

"Heaven and earth will pass away, but
my words will not pass away."

—LUKE 21:33

One of the saddest things I ever heard my mother say was a reflection on the pain that nagged at her heart. It was all about loss—all that had passed and was gone, all the joys of her childhood, the world that would never be again, and the people who had fallen silent. "I just miss everybody," she said. And now we miss her, as someday, our children will miss us.

This life is precious, but Jesus says that all of it will pass away. It is hard for us to accept, but we really have no choice.

But this passing is only the beginning. For Jesus adds, "my words will not pass away." The love of God lasts, brings life to all that we see, and reaches into another glorious eternal life that we can't see yet.

Heavenly Father, enrich my heart with hope in the everlasting joys you promise.

November 26

Sons are indeed a heritage from the L<small>ORD</small>,
the fruit of the womb a reward.
—P<small>SALM</small> 127:3

Pregnant again, I heard the new baby's heartbeat for the first time the other day. The midwife worked her probe around, and we listened to blood and gurgles from my own body until—there it was. Whooshing and beating hard, growing fast, deep within.

I'd heard the sound before, and I knew I was pregnant, but it was thrilling nonetheless, thrilling because God had gifted the world with one more blessing.

Lord God, thank you for the blessing of children—all children—and I pray for all those who care for them. Give them patience and strength.

By contrast, the fruit of the Spirit is love,
joy, peace, patience, kindness, generosity,
faithfulness, gentleness, and self-control.
There is no law against such things.

—GALATIANS 5:22–23

As a writer, one of the things I've noticed is that readers are hardly ever moved to tell you what they think unless they're annoyed.

In other words, I receive much more negative mail than positive, not because most people dislike what I write (at least I hope not!) but rather because anger and disagreement are more powerful motivators to action than are satisfaction and agreement.

As it is in the rest of life, I think. Am I more likely to speak up, even to my own family members, if I have a criticism or complaint—or if I have something kind to say?

God of love, guard my tongue, and help me speak kindly to others.

November 28

Now the Lord is the Spirit, and where the
Spirit of the Lord is, there is freedom.
—2 Corinthians 3:17

It can be very easy for people of faith to fall into a trap. Faith and religion involve traditions and rules. Religion often has to do with regulations that constrain us.

But maybe not. When I take the time to actually listen to Jesus in the Gospels, to really think about what Paul has to say about the life of disciples, I see that the opposite is really true.

The firm, solid grounding is Jesus: his love for us and our love for him. And that, the message seems to be, leads to new things, new life, and freedom.

Am I free?

Jesus, free my heart, burdened by sin. Send your Spirit to free me, constrained as I still am by the world's expectations.

November 29

If any of you is lacking in wisdom, ask
God, who gives to all generously and
ungrudgingly, and it will be given you.

—JAMES 1:5

My daughter has many talents. She is a good
musician, she's intelligent, an enthusiastic
actress, and a surprisingly good basketball player.

But she can't sing as well as her friend Hannah
can, and it irks her. In fact, I suspect that she might
be willing to give up everything else if only she could
sing like Hannah.

It can be a challenge to accept who we are. But
anything less is an act of ingratitude to the one who
gave us the gifts in the first place.

*Creator God, thank you for making me who I am.
Teach me to develop my gifts and be grateful for them.*

November 30

"Now when these things begin to take place, stand up and raise your heads, because your redemption is drawing near."

—LUKE 21:28

When I lived in Florida, Advent and Christmas always caught me by surprise. I did, indeed, own a calendar, but there's just something about palm trees, balmy skies, and wearing shorts that conspires against that particular holiday spirit.

I don't want to be caught by surprise this year, because even though the weather here is cold, plenty of other attractions conspire to distract me. So what will I do? I'll forget about Christmas, first of all, and I'll consider the gift that the Advent season can bring me: four weeks to contemplate what the coming of Jesus means in my life. I'll try not to sleep through it. I'll try, as Jesus tells me, to stay awake to the possibilities that the present holds.

Loving God, help me find the space to prepare myself for this holy season of Advent.

December

December 1

Besides this, you know what time it is, how it is now the moment for you to wake from sleep. For salvation is nearer to us now than when we became believers.

—ROMANS 13:11

After a couple of decades of parenting, I'm not always as attentive as I once was. There are times, for example, when I think if the next words I'm going to hear are "What's for dinner?" (for the 2,765th time since 1989), I'll fade out.

Only to be surprised by something else—some unexpected, delightful good news, perhaps. Most of us have done Advent and Christmas a lot of times. We may not expect to be surprised anymore.

But God has his ways.

Lord Jesus, I set aside my own expectations and open myself to surprise.

December 2

Pray for the peace of Jerusalem:
"May they prosper who love you.
Peace be within your walls,
and security within your towers."
For the sake of my relatives and friends
I will say, "Peace be within you."

—PSALM 122:6–8

The ancient voices yearn for peace. They echo across centuries to the present day. Where is it?

In response, God promises that peace will come, for it is his will.

In our homes, in our world, in our hearts: "Thy will be done." Bring us peace.

Loving God, here is the part of my life where there is turmoil. Give us your peace.

December 3

Give the king your justice, O God,
and your righteousness to a king's son . . .

For he delivers the needy when they call,
the poor and those who have no helper.
He has pity on the weak and the needy,
and saves the lives of the needy.

—Psalm 72:1, 11–13

We prepare to celebrate the coming of our king, to try to straighten the way for him. We open our hearts to his rule—for look what it promises.

As the psalmist indicates, our Savior, King, and Messiah promises much: to deliver the poor, the weak, and the needy. But no king works alone. Our king was explicit about this as he called his disciples and sent them forth to continue his work on earth: Whatever they would do for those poor, they would do for him.

We need our king. We open our hearts to his reign. But reigning with him means more than wielding a scepter. In fact, it doesn't seem to mean that at all, we realize, as we set out on the road in his service.

*Come reign in my life and my world. Thank you
for the privilege of serving the poor, nourished and
strengthened by you.*

December 4

One thing I asked of the LORD,
that will I seek after:
to live in the house of the LORD
all the days of my life,
to behold the beauty of the LORD,
and to inquire in his temple.

—PSALM 27:4

Even though I'm not the queen of holiday parties or particularly obsessed with decoration, as Christmas creeps closer, I do find myself getting tense. I have five children, a husband, and other family members to prepare gifts for; there are school and church programs; there is travel; there are visitors.

But is there time to contemplate the beauty of the Lord?

Loving God, in quiet, I rest in contemplation of your great love.

December 5

"But so that you may know that the Son of Man has
authority on earth to forgive sins"—he said to the
one who was paralyzed—"I say to you, stand up
and take your bed and go to your home."

—LUKE 5:24

Paralysis of the body is the issue here, but I can't
help but think about paralyzed souls, as well. God
created me to journey to him, to grow in intimacy and
holiness. Am I moving?

Or am I paralyzed by my sins? Habits? Fears?

Whatever stops my motion, I hear Jesus' voice:
Rise. Walk.

*Jesus, heal whatever is paralyzing me, and lead my
steps to you.*

December 6

ST. NICHOLAS OF MYRA

"But when you give alms, do not let your left hand
know what your right hand is doing, so that
your alms may be done in secret; and your Father
who sees in secret will reward you."

—MATTHEW 6:3–4

There are countless stories and legends about the deeds of St. Nicholas, a bishop of Myra, in what's now Turkey, back in the fourth century.

I suppose the most well-known is that of the dowry. A man was too poor to provide dowries for his daughters, so Bishop Nicholas found ways to get the needed funds to the family, in secret. The thing I like about the story is that Nicholas was so determined to be anonymous in his giving that for the last daughter, he supposedly dropped the bag of cash down the chimney.

It gives me something to think about. In this season of gift giving, is my heart truly centered on others, or do I give in order to impress?

*Loving God, I pray for a spirit of humble generosity
as I share the blessings you have showered on me.*

December 7

St. Ambrose

"I am the good shepherd. The good shepherd
lays down his life for the sheep."
—John 10:11

I love the story of St. Ambrose's election as bishop of Milan. It's amazing because he wasn't even a baptized Christian at the time.

He was governor of Milan. And when a vacancy occurred, the people, by acclamation, called him to be bishop. He declined, of course, but then decided that perhaps the Spirit of God was working through the people after all, and within a few days, he'd been initiated into the Church, ordained, and consecrated a bishop. He became one of the wisest, most courageous bishops of the period.

It gives me reason to reflect, once again, on God's unusual ways and on the absolute importance of being totally open to God's calls for me—or others—from whatever direction and in whatever form.

Lord God, open my heart to your call. Open my eyes to the possibilities you have for me and for those around me.

December 8

IMMACULATE CONCEPTION

In the sixth month the angel Gabriel was sent
by God to a town in Galilee called Nazareth,
to a virgin engaged to a man whose name was
Joseph, of the house of David. The virgin's
name was Mary. And he came to her and said,
"Greetings, favored one! The Lord is with you."

—LUKE 1:26–28

God gave Mary a great gift, but a necessary one.
It was simply what she needed in order to do his
will—the grace of redemption.

God chooses each of us, too. We live in a hurting
world that yearns for the healing touch of God's love.
It seems beyond us.

But I have to remember this as well: If God wishes
me to be a part of this great work, he will give me the
gifts I need to do it, and I have Mary's prayer and witness to guide me along the way.

*God of love, I come to do your will, trusting that you
will strengthen me with your grace.*

December 9

Have you not known? Have you not heard? The LORD is the everlasting God, the Creator of the ends of the earth. He does not faint or grow weary; his understanding is unsearchable. He gives power to the faint, and strengthens the powerless.

—ISAIAH 40:28–29

This time of year can be exhausting, especially for a lone ranger like me, who, in her heart, doesn't think that anyone else can really do anything right and has some sort of weird pride in pulling celebrations together solely on her own power.

How silly. How prideful. How exhausting.

It's not just true for holiday doings; it's true for the rest of life. Asking for help isn't on anyone's list of sins, as far as I know, while pride is on the top of most of them.

Lord, there are parts of my life in which I need help. Dispel my pride, and strengthen me to seek help when I need it.

December 10

"Therefore you also must be ready, for the Son
of Man is coming at an unexpected hour."
—MATTHEW 24:44

When I taught high school, I taught all levels,
so I got a clear vision of how teens grow and
change over those four years.

The most striking change would occur midway through the junior year when you could see the awareness descend, as they contemplated SAT scores, college brochures, and the past two years of wasted time. Suddenly they were thinking: this counts.

It matters. There's a reason I've been here, doing all these things, making the choices I have made. And the choices all add up.

This counts.

*Jesus, thank you for every day, every hour of my
life. May I use the gift of time with an eye toward
your coming.*

December 11

Be patient, therefore, beloved, until the coming
of the Lord. The farmer waits for the precious
crop from the earth, being patient with it until
it receives the early and the late rains. You also
must be patient. Strengthen your hearts, for the
coming of the Lord is near.

—JAMES 5:7–8

When I was about six years old, a present wrapped
in white paper awaited me under the Christmas
tree. Peeking under the paper, I could see a white box.
Well, I remember reasoning: white paper—white box.
If I open it, and then just put it back under the tree, no
one will be able to tell what I've done.

It didn't work.

But in the end, the only one who was hurt was
me. Impatient, I had ruined the greater surprise.

As I wait for the fullness of the Lord, I hope I don't
spoil the wonders awaiting me by seeking momentary
pleasures.

*Lord Jesus, teach me to wait for the fullness of your
presence with patience.*

December 12

OUR LADY OF GUADALUPE

A great portent appeared in heaven: a woman
clothed with the sun, with the moon under her
feet, and on her head a crown of twelve stars.
She was pregnant and was crying out in birthpangs,
in the agony of giving birth.
—REVELATION 12:1–2

When our Lady appeared to Juan Diego, she
appeared as one of his own: a native woman,
sharing the tint of his people's skin and wearing their
style of dress.

The Son she bore had come to bring the Good
News of love and justice to all, unconfined and unre-
stricted. He was one like us in all things, at all times.

*Jesus, mold my life so that it might reflect the
Good News of justice and peace brought to the
entire world.*

A voice cries out:
"In the wilderness prepare the way of the LORD,
make straight in the desert a highway for our God.
Every valley shall be lifted up,
and every mountain and hill be made low;
the uneven ground shall become level,
and the rough places a plain."

—ISAIAH 40:3–4

As a college student, I spent some time in the mountains of Kentucky, working as a volunteer. Part of what we did was run a vacation bible school. Every morning, we rode a small bus through the hollows and up the hills, picking up children, and every afternoon, we would take them back.

It could be a harrowing trip. How I wished at times for the road to be made straight. Heaven knows what would come at us from around the curve. It seemed that, at any moment, we could be thrown off those sharp turns, and our lives would be lost.

On those curved, steep roads, fear replaced any joy that might lie at the end of the journey.

Lord, make straight and smooth the ways of my heart, so I might focus on your presence.

December 14

St. John of the Cross

Jesus said to them, "Prophets are not without
honor except in their own country and in their
own house." And he did not do many deeds of
power there, because of their unbelief.

—MATTHEW 13:57–58

St. John of the Cross's story is astonishing, since
he was locked up, imprisoned, and silenced not
once but twice by members of his own religious
community.

It's the same story lived by Jesus and by so many
of his disciples in the centuries since. Somehow, those
most entrenched in religious organizations often have
the hardest time seeing truth when it speaks to them.

What threatens us so? What have I got to lose by
recognizing the possibility of God's presence in front
of me, no matter how uncomfortable it might make
me feel?

*God of love, open my eyes to the prophets and saints
in my world today.*

For his anger is but for a moment;
his favor is for a lifetime.
Weeping may linger for the night,
but joy comes with the morning.

—PSALM 30:5

Psychologists and others who study human beings and their behavior tell us that holiday seasons are, ironically, times at which some people feel the worst.

Loss is one of the reasons.

Not all families are intact. More people than we can imagine are wondering how they can face these days without a certain loved one. And some are just mourning times that are past, never to return.

God of comfort, I pray for all those dealing with loss. Open my eyes to their pain, and give me the courage to reach out.

December 16

There was a man sent from God, whose name was John. He came as a witness to testify to the light, so that all might believe through him. He himself was not the light, but he came to testify to the light. The true light, which enlightens everyone, was coming into the world.

—JOHN 1:6–9

Whether I go in or out, I'm surrounded by stuff. Decorations. Music. Lights, trees, and flowers. Sometimes it can seem a bit much. At those times, I slow myself down and remember that no matter how gaudy, how overdone, or even how misused, most of what surrounds me has its roots in something real and true. I can let it distract me, or I can let it bring me closer.

In a tree, I see life and redemption, as the stem from Jesse's root—Jesus' family tree—grows to save me from the sin that first took root in another garden. In gifts, I see the gift of God's Son, as well as the gift of the people who will receive these presents. In all the lights, everywhere, I see darkness overcome.

Jesus, may I be able to see you in all things.

December 17

"My soul magnifies the Lord,
and my spirit rejoices in God my Savior, . . .
He has shown strength with his arm;
he has scattered the proud in the
thoughts of their hearts.
He has brought down the powerful
from their thrones,
and lifted up the lowly;
he has filled the hungry with good things,
and sent the rich away empty."

—LUKE 1:46–47, 51–53

I force myself to look beyond myself, even beyond my own family, to ponder this.

Jesus comes, not simply to reassure me, forgive me, and give me comfort. It's so clear that he comes for reasons that have something to do with the entire world and every person in it.

Justice. Peace. Mercy. The world as God would have it, as God created it to be. My soul magnifies the Lord—for me, for those I know, and for the whole world.

All-powerful God, may all hearts open to your coming.

December 18

Now the birth of Jesus the Messiah took place in this way. When his mother Mary had been engaged to Joseph, but before they lived together, she was found to be with child from the Holy Spirit. Her husband Joseph, being a righteous man and unwilling to expose her to public disgrace, planned to dismiss her quietly.

—MATTHEW 1:18–19

What a harrowing situation. The few lines I read in the Gospels can't possibly convey the weight of the situation on the young woman Mary and the undoubtedly perplexed, good-hearted Joseph.

It's at these shameful moments that we sometimes decide to push God's will aside. Not now. Not this time. It would just be too embarrassing. Everyone would know that I'm not perfect, that my family is flawed, that we're not a greeting-card image come to life.

Well. Would that really be such a terrible thing—for a disciple?

Loving God, strengthen me to accept my life and my family as we are, and to accept your power to use everything for good.

December 19

When the men had come to him, they said, "John the Baptist has sent us to you to ask, 'Are you the one who is to come, or are we to wait for another?'" Jesus had just then cured many people of diseases, plagues, and evil spirits, and had given sight to many who were blind. And he answered them, "Go and tell John what you have seen and heard: the blind receive their sight, the lame walk, the lepers are cleansed, the deaf hear, the dead are raised, the poor have good news brought to them."

—LUKE 7:20–22

I walk into the living room, and I can tell who's been here. The television remote is on the floor: Katie. Blocks spilled over the carpet: Joseph. An empty diet soda can: me. The television turned to ESPN: my husband. Huge tennis shoes sitting by the couch: Christopher or David.

Every presence is accompanied by signs of who's been here.

Lord Jesus, I contemplate, with joy, the signs of your presence in the world.

December 20

I will greatly rejoice in the LORD,
  my whole being shall exult in my God;
for he has clothed me with the garments of salvation,
  he has covered me with the robe of righteousness,
    as a bridegroom decks himself with a garland,
    and as a bride adorns herself with her jewels.

—ISAIAH 61:10

For the past couple of years, makeover shows have been all the rage on television. The point of all of them is that changing your physical appearance (or that of your home) will result in a new you, which will then give you loads of happiness.

So who do I believe—the makeover culture or God?

During this time of year, I hear a lot about joy. What's the source of mine?

Lord Jesus, clothe me with joy.

December 21

Joseph also went from the town of Nazareth
in Galilee to Judea, to the city of David called
Bethlehem, because he was descended from
the house and family of David. He went to be
registered with Mary, to whom he was engaged
and who was expecting a child.

—LUKE 2:4–5

Do you remember when you were pregnant and
you lay sleepless in the night, wondering who
your baby was and when she would come? You could
feel tiny feet pushing on your ribs and even see tiny
elbows and knees skimming under your tightly
stretched skin.

This is what Mary felt, when she ran her hands
over her belly while her restless baby decided to wake
up—when Mama would most like to sleep.

Emmanuel.

Loving God, I contemplate your profound love.

December 22

Immediately his mouth was opened and his tongue freed, and he began to speak, praising God.
—LUKE 1:64

Poor Zechariah, speechless during the most miraculous months of his long life. Struck mute, unable to speak of the joy of his wife Elizabeth's pregnancy.

The loss and restoration of Zechariah's speech were related to his acceptance of God's will. The angel Gabriel took his speech because Zechariah expressed doubt, and it was restored because he gave the child the name God had chosen: John.

My own doubt can make me speechless. When I fail to trust the truth of God's word, I'm rendered speechless in the face of challenges. And when I finally do decide to trust, the funniest thing happens: I can speak again.

Lord, help me trust you and speak the truth fearlessly.

December 23

Lead me in your truth, and teach me,
for you are the God of my salvation;
for you I wait all day long.
—PSALM 25:5

After more than a year, the baby, like a monk praying in his stall in a darkened chapel, insists on keeping vigil every night.

Oh, if I'd been stricter with him when he was smaller, we wouldn't be in this predicament, I know. But I wasn't, and so here we are: every night, the baby named Joseph stays awake for as long as possible and wakes up at least once or twice after that to assure himself of the presence of those he knows love him. He is nothing if not vigilant about that.

The Advent stance of vigilance and waiting is one to which we're called to embrace all the time: being awake and alert for signs of our Savior, the one who loves us. And then, secure in his presence, we can rest.

For at least a couple more hours.

Loving God, help us listen for the signs of your love in our midst.

"Blessed be the Lord God of Israel,
for he has looked favorably on
his people and redeemed them."
—LUKE 1:68

T he weight of it is beyond human words, the truth
of this Word made flesh. In the abstract it is a
puzzle. But when we attach the truth to the sight of
a real baby, perhaps the one peering at us over his
father's shoulder in church, or the one on our very
own lap, it is enough to send us reeling.

Oh, how God loves us.

And he comes to us, not to condemn but to save.
Salvation is what we find when we embrace the baby
and let ourselves be embraced in turn. Freedom.
Release from the sins that burden us, a shattering of
the chains that keep us at a careful, regretful distance
from real love and peace.

*Lord God, thank you for the gift of the Word made
flesh. Help me embrace the freedom you bring in
the child Jesus.*

While they were there, the time came for her
to deliver her child. And she gave birth to
her firstborn son and wrapped him in bands
of cloth, and laid him in a manger, because
there was no place for them in the inn.

—LUKE 2:6–7

How ridiculous it would be, upon meeting a newborn infant, to tell the baby just who he is on the basis of that first encounter. That's just not how we deal with human beings. If we want to know people, we don't do so by instructing them on their identity. We do it by watching the person be who he or she is. We listen.

Might we benefit by taking the same approach with Jesus? Rather than struggling to fit all the magnificent attributes of God into the flesh of the infant, would it not be more appropriate to let the infant tell us who he is, not only through the fact of his birth but through his words and actions as he grows?

What, then, will we learn about God when we silence ourselves in awe, and simply listen to his word?

Loving God, may your word be made flesh
in our lives.

December 26

St. Stephen

While they were stoning Stephen, he prayed,
"Lord Jesus, receive my spirit."
—ACTS 7:59

Yesterday we rejoiced over a baby with joyous songs of praise. Today we remember a man crushed to death under the weight of stones. How strange that the Feast of St. Stephen, the first Christian martyr, directly follows the celebration of the Nativity. But maybe not so strange; for even in the stories of Jesus' birth and infancy, we hear intimations of what is to come. The Good News drives Herod into a fit of murderous rage. Mary is told a sword will pierce her heart. John's Gospel tells us the Word is light sent to illumine darkness. Yesterday we celebrated the light. Today we confront the darkness.

We may want to turn away, but Stephen's story calls us back, back to the truth that when we accept the Child, we accept all that he is: not aloof but fully immersed in the world with all its joy and risk. And where he goes, we, like Stephen, can bravely follow in love.

Lord, fill my heart with the courage to love as you do.

December 27

ST. JOHN

In the beginning was the Word, and the Word
was with God, and the Word was God.

—JOHN 1:1

I think of all the words I've spoken, heard, and written during my life. What's all the talking about? To understand, I suppose. And what is the purpose of understanding? Ultimately it is about drawing closer, into deeper communion.

This is why I love St. John's insight of Jesus as the Word become flesh. It makes so much sense, and it is such a gift. I struggle sometimes to understand God. And pondering God in the abstract seems to get me nowhere.

But then, I turn to the Word. God as a baby, a child, a man, a person, speaking the language of people—my language. When I speak, it is because I want others to know me. Is that perhaps why God speaks as well?

Jesus, Word of God, I am listening.

December 28

HOLY INNOCENTS

When Herod saw that he had been tricked by the wise men, he was infuriated, and he sent and killed all the children in and around Bethlehem who were two years old or under, according to the time that he had learned from the wise men.

—MATTHEW 2:16

Herod's fury led to a heinous act, one which swept up innocents in its destructive path.

As is the case with our anger and the way it touches innocent bystanders. Frustrated by difficulties at work, we lash out at the first person we see when we return home.

Perhaps I should try harder to see the face of the child Jesus in all those who are innocent bystanders.

Lord, I pray for all victims of violence and anger, even when the violence and anger are my own.

December 29

Now after they had left, an angel of the Lord
appeared to Joseph in a dream and said, "Get up,
take the child and his mother, and flee to Egypt,
and remain there until I tell you; for Herod is
about to search for the child, to destroy him."
Then Joseph got up, took the child and his
mother by night, and went to Egypt.

—MATTHEW 2:13–14

As he obeyed God's message to him through
a dream, Joseph was able to protect those in
his care.

All around me, the innocent are threatened by
so much. Abortion, hunger, abuse, and poverty take
their toll. The innocent suffer quietly, alone or as part
of a suffering nation. At the same time, in dreams and
beyond, I think that I hear a message. I know what
God wants; it's no mystery. I know that, just as he
worked through Joseph, God can and wants to work
through me to guard the innocent from harm, in
whatever small or great way I can.

Joseph listened and obeyed. Do I listen? Or would
I rather just change the channel and forget?

Lord, open my heart to the cries of the innocent.

Then he went down with them and came to
Nazareth, and was obedient to them. His mother
treasured all these things in her heart.

—LUKE 2:51

A few days after Christmas, we celebrate Joseph,
Mary, and Jesus: the holy family. I would like
my family to be holy, too, but I don't know. My family
is so far from ideal; we are scattered, we are blended,
and we are all such individuals.

But holiness is there: in mutual love, in moments
of grace, in tenacious commitment, and in daily forgiveness.

I think that's holiness. Or at least it's a start.

*Jesus, I pray for my family. May we grow in holiness
and mutual service, in imitation of your holy family.*

December 31

And the Word became flesh and lived among
us, and we have seen his glory, the glory as
of a father's only son, full of grace and truth.

—JOHN 1:14

When I was ten years old, I went outside on the first day of the New Year with a small bottle. I held it up in the air, put the cap on, taped a label on the outside, and wrote "1970" on it. It fascinated me to think that perhaps I could capture a slice of time and keep it forever.

We can't, of course. Another year has passed, and with it countless moments of joy, sorrow, and routine. Those moments fly away, and they can't be captured in a bottle, no matter how hard we try. But I think that what remains—what does, mysteriously, stay with us and grow—is the glory of the Word we've seen this past year. People and moments have come and gone, but God has pitched his dwelling, and he remains with me.

I can take nothing else into the new year, really, except him. And that's enough.

Jesus, thank you for the past year. I pray that I may grow ever closer to you in the next.

LOYOLA & CLASSICS

New editions of some of the most distinguished
Catholic novels of the twentieth century.

Series Editor: Amy Welborn

Mr. Blue by Myles Connolly
Introduction by John Breslin, SJ.
ISBN 0-8294-2131-9 • $11.95

In This House of Brede by Rumer Godden
Introduction by Phyllis Tickle
ISBN 0-8294-2128-9 • $13.95

Helena by Evelyn Waugh
Introduction by George Weigel
ISBN 0-8294-2122-X • $12.95

Saint Francis by Nikos Kazantzakis
Introduction by John Michael Talbot
ISBN 0-8294-2129-7 • $13.95

Do Black Patent Leather Shoes Really Reflect Up?
by John R. Powers
Introduction by Tom McGrath
ISBN 0-8294-2143-2 • $12.95

The Last Catholic in America by John R. Powers
Introduction by Andrew Greeley
ISBN 0-8294-2130-0 • $12.95

Vipers' Tangle by François Mauriac
Introduction by Gerard Hopkins
ISBN 0-8294-2211-0 • $13.95

The Edge of Sadness by Edwin O'Connor
Introduction by Ron Hansen
ISBN 0-8294-2123-8 • $13.95

The Devil's Advocate by Morris West
Introduction by Kenneth Woodward
ISBN 0-8294-2156-4 • $12.95

Available at your favorite bookstore, or visit
www.LoyolaBooks.org or call **800.621.1008** to order.